The Eloquent Executive

William Parkhurst brings inside moves to *The Eloquent Executive*. He was an executive in the publishing industry before creating Parkhurst Communications, a New York-based speech and media-training company where his clients include many major corporations and public figures. He lives in New York.

Bob Garratt is a management consultant, Chairman of Media Projects International and Visiting Fellow at the Management School of Imperial College, London. He is Chairman of the Association for Management Education and Development.

Other books for The Successful Manager series:

William Parkhurst

The Eloquent Executive

FONTANA/Collins

First published by Times Books,
a division of Random House, Inc., New York, 1988

First published in Great Britain in 1989 by Fontana Paperbacks
8 Grafton Street, London W1X 3LA

Copyright © William Parkhurst, 1988

Printed and bound in Great Britain by
William Collins Sons & Co. Ltd., Glasgow

Conditions of Sale
This book is sold subject to the condition that
it shall not, by way of trade or otherwise, be
lent, re-sold, hired out or otherwise circulated
without the publisher's prior consent in any
form of binding or cover other than that
in which it is published and without a similar
condition including this condition being
imposed on the subsequent purchaser.

To Carolyn

Acknowledgements

With special thanks to Robert Kimmel, Alan Steinberg, David Shanen, Dr Emmanuel Zane, Geralyn Ross, Sandee Brawarsky, Marge Anderson, Bill Hughes, Mel Kaiser, Andrew Carlin, David Peretz, Peg Bailey, Susan Wernerts Lewis, Thomas Lashnits, Dennis Hermanson, Michael Schwager, my agent, Julian Bach, and especially my editor, Hugh O'Neill.

Contents

Introduction

For many years, clients and colleagues have asked me to recommend a book aimed at helping executives to speak in the tough, no-time-for-anything environment of business life. I discovered that good speaking programmes are usually oratorical in nature, while meeting texts address the important, but not especially pertinent, anthropology of small group communication.

The Eloquent Executive is a speech programme for management people who feel the constant heat of corporate demands, who travel a lot, but who are expected to sound as sharp as they look when they present an idea. The programme works quickly and will provide you with the essentials to improve your presentations dramatically. You will not turn into a rafter-shaking corporate evangelist who leaves the audience in a tearful, ring-kissing frenzy. Such power, like a Boris Becker service, comes from some corner of the cosmos that most of us will never see. I promise, however, to fly you first-class to a place where you will give a sharp, focused presentation and be finished before your audience wants to see you go. In an age where careers can stand or fall on the basis of executive showmanship, you could do a lot worse.

The Eloquent Executive was developed more than a decade ago when I began to train authors for radio and television appearances. Producers demand that guests be able to condense complex ideas into a few powerful sentences, and not lose their cool under constant, antagonistic questioning. Five years later, I expanded the plan to help executives prepare for sales conferences, video presentations, trade shows, panels, seminars, and other situations where executives are required to get up there, be great, and get off. The result is a no-frills, speech-by-numbers programme which does not require a heavy investment of time. Of course, as they say at the outset of all such programmes, the more you put in, the more you take away.

The Eloquent Executive begins with all you need to give a lean, mean platform speech, and you will probably be stunned to see how much better you are in front of an audience. But an executive speaking programme must go beyond the lectern to the conference rooms, business lunches, cocktail parties and even aeroplanes, where ideas are really sold.

If you're in middle management, you probably spend 35 per cent of every work week in meetings. Senior executives are in conference between 50 per cent and 75 per cent of their time in the home office. Too often, we stumble through often impromptu speaking situations with no preparation and minimal results. Yet, if we are asked by the Chamber of Commerce to give a speech two months from now, we become obsessed with the event. *The Eloquent Executive* gives it to you both ways. You can be great as a platform speaker as well as in the more spontaneous firefight of a corporate meeting.

We begin with some basics, then move to the book's three main sections, YOUR MESSAGE, DELIVER! and ONE-TO-ONE.

YOUR MESSAGE shows you how to arrange your material so that delivery – that cataclysmic event sometimes more dreaded than surgery – will be almost easy. The first two chapters get you launched. The introduction is such an important piece of any presentation that I have two chapters on it. Even if you've never written a grocery list, you should be able to piece together a forceful opening to carry you through. The main body of your talk is followed by chapters on 'Visual Eloquence', 'Words with Clout', and 'The Conclusion: your big finish'.

The chapters in the DELIVER! section show you how to claim attention when you speak from notes, how to use and read body language, how to turn your voice into a powertool, and how to use your pre-presentation adrenaline for maximum impact. 'Claiming the Room in the First Thirty Seconds' shows you how to take control, and 'The Cycle of the Presentation' ensures that you keep it. Next comes the all-important Q&A, persuasion, running your own meeting, and a final summary of delivery skills in 'Sounding Like You Mean It'.

The third section, ONE-TO-ONE, deals with the less formal, but probably more critical, corporate speaking environments where an idea can stand or fall over a glass of white wine. 'Head to Head: Effective Presentation to an Individual', 'Motivate!', 'Defending against Criticism Without Appearing Defensive', 'The Business Lunch', 'Cocktails at Seven, Dinner at Eight', 'The Impromptu Meeting', 'The Eloquence of Saying Nothing,' and 'Listening: The Ultimate Weapon' concern speaking to individuals or small groups.

I firmly believe in a 1-2-3 approach to speaking. If you focus your attention on what you're doing and what comes next, you'll be great. I say this with conviction because most business speakers are so awful they should be arrested. They commit every excess in this, or any, book.

The Eloquent Executive is a programme of strategies, not theory. Each chapter provides, in numbered sequence, the precise steps for claiming the room in a given situation, or recovering if someone attacks. Each strategy is followed by an 'Instant Review' for immediate reference. Use it on a plane, during a spare minute before you present, or at any time you need to refresh yourself on the dynamics of a speaking problem. The 'Instant Review', which usually takes no more than fifteen seconds to read, jolts your memory and works up energy before you go on.

Do your homework. There is no substitute for substance.

Basic Training

Whether you're arguing for better inventory control in a meeting of five people, or unveiling the new corporate logo before a banquet audience of 1500, certain basics apply.

1 Executive speaking is aggressive: Speaking requires an attitude not unlike competitive sport. Always visualize a successful outcome and move forward, one piece of the talk at a time, thinking hard about what's going on in your present tense. The more you push yourself, and compete with your last performance, the better you will speak.

2 Don't wing it: All effective presentations are grounded in preparation and substance. Even if you have a boss who throws impromptu meetings and puts you on the spot, it all comes down to being ready.

3 Preparation does to fear what flyspray does to a fly: This is not to make light of people's fear of public speaking, or the questionnaires where they report being more afraid of it than of death. However, most executives do not have clinically-diagnosed phobias, and you should take it as a given that the more you prepare the less you fear, and the more you fear, the more rehearsal you need.

4 Prioritize your preparation: Most of the 12,000 or so meetings you will attend in your working career are a colossal waste of time. But the 10 per cent that count require a supercharged mindset, an alertness, presence and elevation of energy which deserve a rating system in your business life. Think concretely in terms of A, B, C and D meetings. A speech, of course, always gets an A rating.

5 Develop rituals around your top category: Don't make these rituals so elaborate that you can't deal with them, but the idea is to crystallize your thinking on important presentations. You might put aside a special suit that you wear only for A meetings and speeches, and keep it in a special part of your closet. Perhaps it's more personal, like dinner at a special restaurant when the job is done. You decide.

6 Look great: Record executives who meet their rock-star clients in an Armani linen jacket, or the sports agent in tennis whites, are as much in uniform as the marketing vice-president in a smart suit. Your organization or industry's code is set in steel and we're not in an era that adores casual eccentricity. You will always present your ideas more effectively if you are dressed as well as you can be.

For a time, corporate women endured an unspoken dictum that they had to dress as severely as turn-of-the-century school-mistresses or, worse, like men. While some companies still push shapeless dark suits and those uninspiring bows as regulation conference room attire, a saner, more professional look prevails today. Corporations seem to have discovered that good taste extends to silk dresses, open-toed shoes, pastels and attractive make-up. Trouser suits are about as welcome as men in drag.

7 Always keep your mind directly on the material: Assessing your performance as you go through a talk will give you vertigo and kill any hope you had of being good. Don't think about the audience, the boss, the drink you're going to have afterwards, or the plane ride home. Keep all your attention and energy on the material.

8 Check out the room when you can: To a person giving a set speech to the PTA, seating arrangements are irrelevant. The executive speaker, however, has a lot more to think about. The audio-visual hardware has to be in place, and the way people are arranged has a direct bearing on the outcome and style of the presentation (see 'Audience Analysis' p. 20).

9 Communicate, don't educate!: Most business speakers feel they have to present sufficient minutiae to give everyone, including waiters and waitresses, doctorate material in the subject matter. Put the boring details on a hand-out sheet and get down to the business of being effective. The mind can take only the essentials, and a short time after the talk your audience will be hard-pressed to remember anything you said. But they'll remember the way you said it.

10 Stage presence is acting, so act!: The personality you put across is the result of posture, body language, facial expression, vocal range, and other things you can learn and practise. Don't leave these mechanics to chance.

11 Remembering names is part of the job: Here is another instance where business speaking differs dramatically from run-of-the-mill prepared talks. The audience in a corporate environment has teeth. 'Cocktails at Seven' (p. 129) offers some tricks for remembering names.

12 Don't read a written speech: Except in rare cases where the public is involved and an advance copy of the text has to be provided to the press, or where the speaker is very experienced, this rule should be considered gospel. Most of us simply can't pull it off.

13 Start on time, end on time: Even the flakiest actors and actresses get to work on time. It's considered unprofessional, and in very poor taste, to do otherwise. In business, arriving late puts us on the defensive. When you have to give an excuse for your behaviour, your position and credibility are weakened.

Running over time is just plain crazy. Don't do it under any circumstances.

14 Humour: When in doubt, don't!: Most comedy clubs have an audition night where anyone can get up and do a little routine. If you check the alley outside the exit, you'll find the bruised bodies of class clowns, barroom John Cleeses and Julie Walterses along with other 'naturals' who thought they couldn't miss.

Humour is one of the best tools, but it should be approached like the loaded gun it is. You can offend the Chief Executive's spouse or make a topical joke which your audience takes personally. You can tell a great story which everyone has heard. You're better off starting with ad-libbed chunks of wit than trying to deliver prepared lines.

15 Understand what your voice can do: Your voice is an instrument that can be used to command, coax, elicit sympathy, overpower opposition, or perform a thousand other tasks. Understanding how to optimize your vocal range is one of the best gifts you can give yourself. 'Powervoicing' (p. 75) will start you off.

16 Never ask the audience for sympathy: They don't, and shouldn't, want to know about your discomfort. Begging their indulgence is like asking someone you've just met for money. Don't do it.

17 Know your introduction and conclusion cold: You shouldn't ever *memorize*. That's even worse than reading from a prepared text. You should, however, know everything you're going to say at the top and bottom of a talk well enough to recite it in your sleep. This ensures that you'll launch yourself well and come in for a smooth landing, and brings truck-loads of confidence.

Instant Review

1 Think aggressively when you speak
2 Don't wing it
3 Preparation zaps fear
4 Prioritize your preparation
5 Develop rituals around important presentations
6 Look great
7 Stay focused on the material
8 Check out the room ahead of time
9 Communicate, don't educate
10 Stage presence is an acting job
11 Remember names
12 Don't read a written speech
13 Start on time, end on time
14 Humour: When in doubt, don't!
15 Know your voice
16 Never ask the audience for sympathy
17 Know your introduction and conclusion cold

The Playing Fields

Control is often a function of setting. Where you speak always has a direct influence on your talk. Here are tips for speaking in five of the most typical business environments:

1 The conference room: Stand up if it's a formal presentation. You'll have more control. Stand where you can make comfortable eye contact with as many of those attending as possible. Speak from either of the ends, or the centre of one side. Be opposite the most powerful participants so you can play to them.

2 The theatrical layout: This is the common auditorium setting with you on stage or at the bottom of a hill of rows. This arrangement is fine for an informational presentation, a platform speech, a firm lecture, or any situation where audience participation is at a minimum.

3 Team seating: The audience is broken into small discussion clusters for problem-solving or other functions of high participation. Avoid team seating if you simply want to put the word out or feel the constraints of a short session. Teams are definitely for the longer meetings.

4 Classroom seating: Classroom seating is straight rows of desks or tables separated by aisles. Seminars, lecture-oriented training sessions and other instructional purposes are served by this arrangement.

If you're a pacer who likes to walk and talk at the same time, arrange the tables in a staggered, herringbone fashion so people can keep track of you. A disadvantage is that classroom seating often has everything on the same level, making visuals difficult to introduce and integrate.

5 The senate seating arrangement: Each row has its own elevated level, like the US Senate. The acoustics are usually good in rooms like this and they are designed for modern audiovisual equipment, especially videotape. A drawback is eye contact. If they're elevated, you're down at the bottom of a well looking up at your audience. Once you get accustomed to this pattern, however, it becomes almost intimate and makes it easy to deliver any kind of message.

Instant Review

Before you speak, check out the room.

1 The conference room: take a speaking position where everyone can see you. Speak either from the end of the table, near people with power, or in the centre of one of the sides.

2 Theatrical seating: perfect for speeches involving minimal audience participation. Not good for give-and-take situations.

3 Team seating: Little clusters of people as part of a larger group. Ideal for any kind of training, participation, problem solving etc.

4 Classroom seating: Good for seminars, training sessions, other instructional goals. Make sure you have a stage not too far above the tables.

5 Senate seating: Takes some getting used to, but adaptable and acoustically good.

Section I: Your Message

Demagogues claim that a lie told with enthusiasm becomes truth, while truth told with hesitation becomes a lie. Fortunately, people catch on, and see through to the core of someone's message; they spot substance or its absence. Substance is what this section is about: your message is you and it has to be credible. A great speaker with nothing to say is just a flamboyant bore. How many times have you seen some fool in a meeting trying to protect his hide or turf, spouting words no one in the room believes?

We begin with audience analysis and a checklist for tailoring your message to the needs of that audience. Next comes writing the words to be spoken. If you want to drive yourself mad, try using florid language in a speech. There are seven steps for getting your presentation drafted; if you follow them, you'll be through with that chore in about an hour.

Your focus is narrowed because the whole message hinges on a single main theme. This alone places you ahead of the corporate pack, for people simply don't know how to keep a topic lean. The introduction to a talk – any talk of any size, anywhere – is so important that we devote two chapters to it. First, we look at the pieces for a room-grabbing introduction. Next come the rules. Master the intro, master the speech. Almost, anyway.

Draft the main body next. It's not especially sexy, but that little thing called substance comes in as your thesis is supported. Visuals (a chapter which can't be avoided) are included in this section rather than in the delivery section. You should write around visual aids, not shoehorn them in as you rehearse. 'Words with Clout' (p. 52) will get you away from the awful corporate clichés forever celebrating a wooden optimism no one feels:

'I take our setback as a *challenge*.'

'The new line gives us an unprecedented opportunity to *forge ahead* and *win the battle*!'

You can kiss that garbage goodbye.

Finally 'Your big finish' (p. 59) deals with the conclusion, which may be the most important part of the talk. You decide, but always finish big and end on an upbeat note.

Audience Analysis

Think hard about the people who will receive your message. Are you addressing senior vice-presidents in your company, or a mixed bag of executives in your field? Will there be other speakers? A Q&A? What is the seating arrangement? You must know the audience, its disposition, its problems and, in the case of small groups, the specific cast. A checklist should eliminate some of the guesswork in your evaluation:

1 Why are they there? What is the common social or occupational bond that has brought them to the room to hear you? Are they happy to receive your information or is this a rote political event which their corporate survival dictates?

2 Do they know anything about your subject? Jargonizing and overeducating are bad form. If they're new to the subject, they'll still be novices when they leave the room.

3 What are the minimum and maximum they can absorb? Have a firm idea of what you want to cover, how much you think they can realistically absorb, and put minutiae on a hand-out sheet.

4 How educated are they?

5 What is the proportion of women to men? Besides providing you with a profile of the audience, knowledge of women to men governs your use of personal pronouns. If it's all male, 'he' will do fine. For the most part, you'll have to mix it up.

6 What is the average age? Age governs most things. You simply have to know.

7 What attitudes do they have about your topic? Finance people like numbers. Personnel executives think of slots and the cost of filling them with people. Every member of your audience will evaluate your presentation in terms of his or her corporate agenda.

8 What is their socio-economic level? Where they grew up isn't as important as where they live now. Never be so naïve as to assume it doesn't matter.

9 What are their common problems? Has everyone in the room had to contend with a new computer system right after they got used to last year's new computer system? Did the Chief Executive retire, leaving them with a lot of uncertainty? Their problems concern them constantly, and should concern you as you prepare your talk.

10 Is there a Q&A? How long? Only bad speakers ramble on, formally or informally. Pace yourself and always prepare for a Q&A, even if you are told there will not be one.

Instant Review

1 Why are they there?
2 Do they know anything about your topic?
3 What can you expect to teach them?
4 How educated are they?
5 What is the proportion of women to men?
6 Average age?
7 What are their attitudes about your subject?
8 Economic level?
9 Do you address their common problems?
10 Will there be a Q&A? If so, how long?

The Quick Way to Write Your Presentation

1 Brainstorm constantly: Ideas rarely flow predictably. They come to you in hypnogogic form as you wake up, or crystallize as you drive to work. Keep a notebook or an index card within reach and capture any idea that visits.

2 Write everything for your talk in one single session: Jot. It doesn't matter whether you scribble, type or write in whole sentences. Everything should find its way into your notes in an hour or less. Put down whatever occurs to you and pay no attention to form, order or style.

3 Add current facts as they relate to your audience profile: A short item from a trade journal may fit beautifully into your notes, but check that the journal is familiar to your audience.

4 Transfer your notes to cards and prioritize: Talk the speech through as though you're having a conversation with a friend in a bar. Don't write out the text yet. Business presentations call for just the facts and their illustrations, so be selective about what stays and goes. Put the cards in an order that makes sense to you.

5 Now write it all in plain conversational language: 'Writing' can be interpreted in many ways. You may be doing so well talking it through from your notes that you never get to putting it down word for word. Or you may be more secure in fashioning a text from your notes. When the notes are in the right order, the talk will write itself.

6 Sculpt the language: Your introduction and conclusion, though delivered from notes, require precision. You have to know them as well as your own name. The main body of the talk should be packed with information which supports your main thesis logically and defends against counter-attack.

Use High Impact words and phrases (see 'Words with Clout', p. 52), remembering that the language of business must convey decisiveness, force and a constant attention to the specifics of profit.

7 Develop a topic outline: You read it right. Do the text first, *then* make the outline. Audiences are very childish about your attention. They want it all. This means a minimum of contact with source material. Work from a spare outline which highlights your main points. The rest has to be in your head.

Example: Underground economy hits us all in the pocket – government loses 90 billion, you (at 100K) lose a hundred a week – courts clogged, enforcement nil – major impact on food industry etc.

There are two kinds of topical outline:

(a) *The rehearsal outline* highlights all topics and subtopics. Use it only for practice.

(b) *The skeletal outline* is your final presentation roadmap and should be very spare. A few broad headings to remind you where you're going frees you for the all-important eye contact with your audience.

Of course, a lean skeletal outline underscores a well-rehearsed talk. There are many steps one can skip but rehearsal is, unfortunately, not among them.

Instant Review

1 Brainstorm constantly, jot down ideas
2 Write everything in one session
3 Update your facts to make them relevant and timely
4 Transfer your notes to cards and prioritize
5 Write a whole draft in plain, conversational language, either talking it through or spelling it out
6 Sculpt the language
7 Develop a topic outline; first in detailed rehearsal form, later as a skeletal roadmap

---

Preparing a Room-Grabbing Introduction: The Pieces

The known importance of the introduction as the foundation of the talk is a stumbling block to its effective preparation. An 'I've got to be greater than great!' mentality sets in to burn up your time and sabotage your effort.

The next two chapters de-mystify the introduction, so you can zip through it and get to the main body and conclusion. First, we'll look under the bonnet and probe through the wires, where we find that there really isn't so much to an introduction after all. It should last three minutes or less and accomplish five goals:

(a) Command audience attention
(b) Make a one-to-one connection
(c) Establish your credibility
(d) State your central idea emphatically
(e) Express your view of your central idea

Commanding audience attention

We are emotional creatures. We hunger, thirst, lust, laugh, and cry – and we're always greedy children who want to know what's in it for us. Place yourself in your audience and keep the emotional aspects of the human character in focus as you prepare your introduction. Despite the quantitative, bottom-line, demands-of-a-business presentation, you command attention when you analyse your audience and show them that you are addressing their greed.

Don't tax yourself with having to keep everyone's attention at all times. They'll tune in and out depending on how much of what they hear applies to their needs. Someone, however, will always be with you and it is to that person, real or imaginary, individual or collective, that you address your introduction.

Here are six devices for commanding attention. Use one or more to match your particular delivery style:

(a) The captivating statement

In 1975, eleven people invested ten thousand dollars each in my company. Last year, they became millionaires.

The captivating statement should jolt your audience a bit, make them glad something didn't happen to them, or envious that it happened to someone else. It should press gently on the nerves, implying a near miss, but don't try to do too much or you'll slip into overkill.

If you're illustrating good news, seduce them with the thought that they should soon be able to try it themselves with the same positive results. If it's bad news, there should be a feeling of relief. Sometimes you can take them on a thrill ride:

'If you invested ten thousand dollars of your money with me in 1975, I'd have lost it all on you by 1980 . . . (pause) . . . and offered it back to you with a little interest in 1981 . . . (pause) . . . And if you went against the advice of your sane friends and stayed with me, I'd have made you a millionaire this year.'

Most captivating statements do the job in a single declarative sentence:

'Eight of us here today will be dead by this date next year.'

But be warned: captivating statements are easily overdone, so make sure your supporting text lives up to the promise of the statement.

Their advantage is that they nearly always work.

(b) Statistical chorus line

Last Christmas, 31,000 assembly workers in this state were able to fill their kids' stockings because there was plenty of work. All but 2500 of those 31,000 workers are unemployed today and, thanks to the Governor, they will be joined by another 10,000 or more next Christmas Eve. I employ 440 people whom I can no longer afford to pay because of the capital equipment tax. I'm leaving too. Merry Christmas, Governor.

A statistical chorus line looks beyond numbers to their human applications and combines the two elements, but be certain that your statistics will withstand the arguments of your opponents.

Examine the larger picture to ensure that you're emphasizing a valid point, rather than engaging in a rhetorical martial art which could be construed as a cheap shot. By using numbers, you are in inherently familiar territory. By applying them, you have saved your audience the trouble of sorting out the statistics.

(c) Provocative questions: Whether rhetorical or direct, these wake an audience up:

> 'Anyone here interested in an extra thousand a week, no strings attached?'
>
> *or*
>
> 'What does the colour red have to do with employee productivity?'
>
> *or*
>
> 'If I told you you wouldn't have to pay a dime for your childrens' education, what name would you call me?'

(d) Quotations

> 'Let us all be happy to live within our means, even if we have to borrow the money to do it.'
>
> *Charles Farrar Browne*

> 'There never was a war of arms that was not merely the extension of a preceding war of commerce grown fiercer until the weapons of commerce seemed no longer significantly deadly.'
>
> *Hugh L. Johnson, 1935*

Shakespeare once said . . . Henry Ford put our situation this way . . . a quotation takes the listener directly into the central theme of the talk. It can be effective anywhere in the text, so long as it is not overused. But try to stay away from tired old quotes, and don't put one in the introduction when it really belongs in the conclusion.

(e) Contextual humour: Never tell a joke. As we've pointed out, humour is precarious ground, but in the right hands it can be a useful device for getting attention.

Humour should come from the context of the workplace. Suppose you're a department head addressing other department heads on employee incentives. One of your peers, George Bennett, began offering hard-to-get sports, theatre, and concert tickets as a motivational device for his subordinates. The plan has worked so well that others, especially Price, middle management's resident sports fanatic, are besieged with pressure from their workers.

Your humour would come from a situation which tapped into a common peer problem:

> 'I'm sure we *all* want to congratulate George Bennett for the brilliant idea that caused us all to face mutiny . . . (pause) . . . I notice Price has applied for a job as a clerk in George's department.'

Or, it's so well-known that the company cars are lemons that even the CEO has joked about the problem openly:

'I especially want to thank the purchasing department for my car. I'm sure the AA will find a way to get it out of Newcastle.'
Keep humour short, and tasteful. There are, as you probably know, two components of any gag: the set-up, and the punch. The set-up is a line or two depicting the ordinary: 'Before John's visit, the car park was filled with Mercedes and Jaguars.' The punch is usually a surprise, or a distortion of reality: 'And the day after he left, they'd all turned into Minis without radios. I don't know how the man does that.'

(f) Visual attention grabbers: If you walk to the edge of the stage and throw a glass of water into the front row, you will certainly get their attention. This is not recommended, but it will work. There are many less dramatic visual attention grabbers.

Suppose you take the stage and remove a pound note from your wallet. You light it and say nothing as it burns in an ash-tray. When it is out, you say: 'This company does that ten thousand times every morning, takes an hour for lunch, and does it another ten thousand times every afternoon.'

You can achieve dramatic results with the careful use of visuals in an introduction, but be warned that visuals are the most gimmicky of attention-getting devices.

Making a one-to-one connection

Never broadcast. Talk to your audience (meeting or platform speech doesn't matter) one-to-one, as though there is no *they*. Act as though the audience is a single co-worker and the two of you are having a drink to talk this thing out. Public speaking is conversation, and it might be better to think of the process as talking rather than speaking. There are five important strategies in making that one-to-one connection:

(a) **Be yourself:** You are asked to speak because someone believes you have a significant bank of ideas. Congratulations. You don't have to become someone else. There's no need to put on a fake character. Whoever you are, let them see you.

(b) **Personal anecdote:** Stories – your stories – which relate to the central theme require no spirit of dazzle or joke-telling ability. A personal experience told in a straightforward manner usually goes much further with a business audience than a lot of theatrics. Tell them why you came to use the product, or how you changed your viewpoint:

> A lot of you feel that biomedical engineering is the end to family life as we know it. I understand that position because, until I joined the company, I felt the same way. Not only did I feel that the technology sounded the death knell for family life, but I thought it dangerous for every organism on the philogenetic scale. Let me tell you why I no longer see things that way.

You're talking to them.

(c) **Put their needs ahead of yours:** Once the one-to-one connection is made, there is plenty of time to address your problems and ideas. In the introduction, address their problems and needs.

(d) Use 'you' more and 'I' less: There's absolutely nothing wrong with 'I'. You will use it constantly. But the intro is a selling job and you sell by showing your client or customer why they need something.

(e) Use the moment after you're introduced for its inherent one-to-one opportunity: As soon as the moderator has reeled off your credits, take a few seconds to humanize your introduction. After a particularly flattering introduction, you might say:

'Thank you, June. I liked that introduction a lot. May I hear it again?' or 'Thanks so much, Bob. I really enjoy coming back to London. We won't talk about cricket, but how about those hockey players?'

It doesn't have to be funny. Just an acknowledgement of something in common serves as a connector before you get into the introduction.

(f) A show of hands: Asking an audience how many present ever did this, or saw that, loosens them up, adds to your information about them, and establishes a link. It makes the conversation a little more intimate.

Establishing your credibility

This essential component is usually provided for you in formal speeches. In meetings, it might be necessary for you to slip it into the introduction:

'In seventeen years of working in industrial relations, I've seen the field undergo three radical changes.'

'My first three years with the company were as a field rep in the far west.'

'My wife doesn't think I'll ever finish, but I am completing my doctorate in particle physics.'

Stating your central idea emphatically

Always be specific in the emphatic statement of your central purpose.

Don't say: 'I'm going to talk to you about computers.' The subject is too broad. You couldn't cover it if you had them in front of you for a week.

Say: 'I'm going to show you software options which will dramatically affect how your company uses computers in the warehousing of three product lines.'

Expressing your view of your central idea

The final sentence of the introduction is a good place to express your view of the central idea. Don't be coy. They always want to know how you feel about your topic. You may not have come to more than a preliminary conclusion. If so, tell them:

'I'm waiting for R&D to complete their tests on this alloy, but right now I'm ready to discontinue the use of aluminium in our components.'

Always be as definite about your view as you possibly can:

'Being good to workers is not some idealist's view of how a factory should be. It's just plain good business. Productivity goes way up and I'll show you why.'

Instant Review

The intro is intimidating because it is the foundation of the presentation. It can eat up the preparation time for the all-important main body and conclusion. But when you examine it, an introduction has only five goals.

1 Command their attention
You can use six different strategies:

    (a) The captivating statement
    (b) The statistical chorus line
    (c) Provocative questions
    (d) Contextual humour
    (e) Quotations
    (f) Visual attention grabbers.

2 Make a one-to-one connection
    (a) Never broadcast; approach the audience as though it's one person and you are talking things over in a bar
    (b) Be yourself
    (c) Personal anecdote
    (d) Put their needs ahead of yours
    (e) A show of hands
    (f) Use 'you' more, 'I' less
    (g) Use the moment after you've been introduced as a one-to-one opportunity.

3 Establish your credibility
Congratulations. Someone thinks you have something important to say. If your credentials and authority are not established by the moderator (and sometimes even when they are) you'll have to find a way to work it into the top of your speech.

4 State your central purpose emphatically
Always be specific and prune your introduction of generalities.

5 State your view of your topic
Don't be coy. Show the audience where you stand.

Preparing a Room-Grabbing Introduction: The Rules

Now that you know the structure of the introduction, there are Do's and Don't's which, when mastered and put into the basic framework, will result in a room-claiming start. The introduction is the only time when you are guaranteed the undivided attention of everyone in the room. If you lose them, they are usually gone for the duration. Despite the threat of such pressure, there is some good news:

1 When you take over at the beginning, the rest is simple: Get them in the first few minutes, and they'll follow you anywhere. A good intro will cover a multitude of content and delivery sins.

2 A strong intro highlights your leadership ability: In fact, you may get more leadership credit than you deserve when senior management people who have barely noticed you, watch you walk to the front of the room and take command.

3 It deals a lethal blow to nervousness: Do well at the beginning and, assuming you are well prepared, anxiety transforms itself into excitement and enthusiasm in your delivery. You won't be tentative for the rest of the presentation.

4 In a great introduction, your personal style becomes an asset: In a strong, honest intro a low-key delivery will be remembered as subtle and in control. A vibrant, enthusiastic style will be perceived as even more so. So long as you are direct, concise and look in control, there is no right or wrong style.

Here are the Big Do's of an effective introduction:

1 Converse at all times: Your tone should be exactly as it is when you speak to a friend. Whether you address a single imaginary person or develop your own system, the language you choose should fit you like a slipper. If you don't use certain words in conversation, don't use them in meetings or on the podium.

2 Be solution-oriented: A businesslike, solution-oriented tone in your introduction establishes instant credibility: 'There are three ways for us to enter the market, and I see only one of them as viable without a major acquisition.'

3 Be precise: Credibility and precision are the same thing in a business presentation. Pack your talk with real information and leave supposition or generalities at home.

Vague: 'Legions of workers have benefited from the new medical coverage since we inaugurated it eighteen or so months ago.'

Precise: 'We inaugurated this programme in January of 1986 and have since insured 4902 employees in our product development division. There have been 51 claims for minor injuries, 14 major trauma injuries, and 3 hospital visits of more than a week's duration. All claims were settled without legal contest.'

4 Be brief: An introduction tells them in a few minutes what they're going to hear, before you connect with your main body. Observe a powerful person in a meeting: he or she comes right to the point, wasting little time on banter. A long statement is weak. A short statement is strong.

Say: 'That's nonsense.'

Don't say: 'I've given considerable thought to the implications of that problem, bearing in mind its many ramifications, and how others in this room may feel about it, and I would have to say it is totally untenable.'

The Big Don't's are bigger in the introduction than in any part of the speech. Here they are:

1 The biggest: don't put too much pressure on your intro: An introduction is a seduction. You can't just stamp your way to success with it. You can put only so much pressure on your delivery or you'll find yourself waiting for a joke to get across, or for a reaction to your carefully-timed, shocking first sentence. When none of it happens, as it often doesn't for ten thousand reasons not having anything to do with you, you'll get thrown and stumble through the rest of the talk. You can't preach, educate or topple them with detail. You can't dazzle with your brilliance yet, because they haven't bought you.

The texture of your introduction must match the rest of the speech, or you have a pinstriped jacket with herringbone lapels. You can get their attention, but you must deliver with the precise tone, force and body language of the main body and conclusion.

2 Never apologize: Do not sell off your credibility with apology or equivocation.

Say: 'In my law practice, I constantly work with cost accountants and they hate tax-deferred investments for three reasons.'

Don't say: 'I'm not really a specialist in cost accounting, but I'll muddle through as best I can.' If you're up there, someone thinks you have the authority to run the show. You have to think so too.

3 Don't use common ground when you expect a negative response.

Say: 'I am alarmed at the prime minister's build-up of Israeli troops in Beirut, and my position has frequently resulted in charges of anti–Semitism which I consider groundless and irrelevant to the issue.'

Don't say: 'I grew up in a Jewish neighbourhood and frequently went to temple with my good friend, Hymie Bernstein. I know, believe me I know, how a lot of you feel about my position on Israeli troops in Beirut.'

4 Don't ask for sympathy or forgiveness: As in: 'I know that some might see what I did as influence peddling, and I admit that the courts ruled against me, but . . .' or, 'I have a terrible cold, so if I seem a little wobbly . . .'

Instead say: 'I don't care, frankly, what the courts found. It's only the first round. I'm a lawyer who collected a fee, not an influence peddler.' As for the cold, say absolutely nothing about your health except perhaps an apology when you sneeze.

5 Don't hedge: As in: 'I'd have to double-check those figures, but . . .'

'I'm not entirely sure of this, but . . .'

'Well, it could go entirely the other way, and I'm not saying I entirely disagree, but . . .'

Say it. We all know there are two sides to an issue and we don't care. We want to hear your side. The only permissible hedge is a question from the audience unrelated to your central theme.

Hedging is simply a way of asking permission to be wrong. You can always say you have not yet seen a specific report, or your opinion could change pending new data. You can always offer the most honest answer: you just can't answer the question or address the issue. But don't join that gutless army who can't bear the pressure of a position. Leadership means taking a stand – and a chance. Right or wrong, in the end you'll get respect.

6 Don't kiss the audience's collective ring
Say: 'I'm very honoured to be here.'

Don't say: 'I'm so in awe of being in the presence of such a distinguished group that I had to ask myself, "what would such accomplished individuals possibly want to hear from me?"'

7 Don't use buzz words hoping your audience will relate to them:
Unless you understand fully the jargon of someone else's industry, avoid buzz words or you risk seeming to try too hard.

8 Beware of offending women and minority groups: Several times
each year, a president, head of state or some other high government official makes a casual remark which deeply offends women or ethnic or minority groups. The headlines blare for days as the dignitary amuses us by trying to explain, er, what he really meant.

We feel superior until a variation of the same thing happens to us. If there is a rule of thumb, it is to avoid even the most broadly interpretive stereotypical references. Blacks don't want you to assume that they are good dancers or athletes. The Japanese fail to see the amusement in Pearl Harbour jokes or the term, 'Ah-so'.

Men are often surprised when, after paying a woman executive all due egalitarian courtesy, they alienate her by referring to a female assistant as 'My girl', as in 'I'll have my girl call your girl

35

and we'll set up a lunch.' Even innocent references to a wife's cooking, or a roll of the eyes to indicate a shrewish mate can cause problems. In meetings, the wrong kind of eye contact with a member of the opposite sex can send mixed signals and threaten the bounds of corporate taste.

9 Don't make promises that can't be delivered in the main body: You should never be so provocative, so flamboyant, or so dynamic that you're making an offer you can't back up later: 'During the next thirty minutes, your life will have changed so much that you'll walk through those doors seeing the world as a very different place.'

10 Don't be too elaborate: Remember not to educate. Any esoteric data should be left for the hand-out sheet, and jargon is never appropriate unless every person in that room works with the terminology every day.

Instant Review

There's good news about introductions, despite the pressure:
1 When you take over at the beginning, the rest is easy
2 A strong intro highlights your leadership ability
3 It deals nervousness a lethal blow
4 In a great introduction, your personal style is an asset

The Big Do's of an effective introduction:
1 Converse at all times
2 Be solution-oriented
3 Be precise
4 Be brief

The Big Don't's:
1 The biggest: Don't put too much pressure on an introduction
2 Never apologize
3 Don't force common ground when you expect a negative response
4 Don't ask the audience for sympathy or forgiveness
5 Don't hedge
6 Don't kiss the audience's ring
7 Don't use buzz words
8 Beware of offending women and minority groups
9 Don't make promises which can't be delivered
10 Don't be too elaborate

The Main Body

Your main body is the workhorse of your presentation. It is not, quite frankly, as inspiring as the introduction or conclusion, for it neither sells you nor leaves them begging for more. The human attention span inevitably drifts until the magical words that signal the conclusion.

However, substance is *the* critical element of any presentation

37

and it is in the long middle that you prove your mettle. The main body gives the audience reason to agree with you; every piece of information you convey must be in support of your argument. A good body has to do seven things:

1 Sustain their interest: You, and not your data, are what holds your audience. You virtually cannot fail when you present a straighforward summary of your material and why you believe in it. If you are enthusiastic, they'll buy you whether they ultimately accept or reject your arguments. Too many speakers try to dazzle with Houdini tactics and overproduced visuals, when all they really need is intense focus and enthusiasm. Sell yourself on your material. After that, visuals do work, but they are secondary

2 Follow a logical order: There must be some sensible framework, some direction where you're taking them with your ideas. There are two basic maps for you to follow:

(a) The **subject** path breaks the topic into its key components, often three parts. As in: 'The bankruptcy occurred for three key reasons: The company was undercapitalized, it failed to expand on time, and the management structure was topheavy with sales people.'

(b) The **chronological** path is especially useful in technical presentations where A must precede B, which must, in turn, come before C. As in: 'Re-tooling for underground pipe manufacture will first require shutting down the Altoona plant. Then, we must make a personnel decision based on which employees to lay off . . .'

3 Be specific: This advice crops up everywhere in High Impact Speaking. In the main body it refers to spareness, with digression only when it makes a spectacular example.

Don't say: 'Countless surveys indicate that the source of the problem is . . .'

Say instead: 'In a survey at St Luke's Hospital in Ketchum, Idaho over a period of twenty years, between 1958 and 1978 . . .'

4 Follow a thread which relates only to your central theme:
Continue to remind your audience of your dominant theme and purpose:

'There are two more reasons why workers who smoke need their own place to do so.'

'Loss of central control is another solid argument against divestiture.'

5 Give them breathing room: Any presentation more than fifteen minutes long, especially if you're the only speaker, requires a break to revive momentum. This is not a dismissal of their attention, but a fortification of it. Don't send them out for coffee before an hour passes, but plan to vary your pace, visual impact, drop your formality for an instant, inject humour, or take some other measure to break it up a bit. Do this every fifteen or twenty minutes, and allow fifteen minutes off in a long talk of between an hour and ninety minutes.

6 Mix solid transitions with supporting arguments: You wouldn't write ten pages without changing paragraphs. In speaking, you need to move from one sub-topic to the next with verbal bridges.

7 Fortify your position against critics: Don't be so cautious that you speak defensively, but all your supporting points should, directly or indirectly, address the main weakness of your central theme.

● **Specialized presentation patterns for meetings**

Meetings, conferences and other internal communications functions often require more specialized organization. Here are five patterns to consider if you're planning to address a small corporate group:

1 The regional pattern: Most large companies constantly shuttle regional executives in and out of the home office. Such ongoing travel lends itself to a geographic organizational approach: 'The new billing system will be phased in over the next six months, and I'll explain how it will affect six zones. In Glasgow . . .'

2 The problem-solution organization: Present a single problem and follow immediately with its solution: 'I can count on losing a full ten per cent of my unskilled and semi-skilled assembly workers every single Monday. I propose three plans for reducing this absenteeism.'

Be concrete and direct. Don't follow a problem with another problem, then blend solutions. It's always one problem at a time in this scheme of organization.

3 The cause/effect order: It is difficult to draw the line between cause/effect and problem solution as you make the decision on how you're going to organize your main body. Cause/effect is especially productive for the more positive highlighting of a new programme, system or organizational effort: 'The new coded application form has resulted in an eight per cent reduction of office turnover during the first year of its use. There are four other benefits to it as well.'

Of course, the cause/effect blueprint is in constant use for the more sinister purpose of laying blame and couching it in Good Of The Compay rhetoric: 'I have to say that the sales department's new telemarketing system has resulted in a barrage of customer complaints and I worry about possible litigation. There are other disasters that result from this programme.'

4 The power-determined order: Getting ahead means that your boss has to see you in control as you present ideas which aren't going to be gratefully received by several labour leaders in attendance. Maybe your department is delivering some news which senior management staff will find annoying. Your more common, acceptable ideas don't belong at the end of the presentation when they're already steaming. Ease in: 'We want very much to come to terms with the welders. Some of these tradesmen have been with us for more than twenty years, and this company has a long tradition of respecting seniority. I think we all agree on that.'

5 The data-grounded order: Sometimes your presentation is all numbers. Let the data determine your order of presentation, moving from the lowest to highest, or vice versa: 'The highest percentage of returns comes from three stores in the south-west at 5.28 per cent of merchandise shipped. Next come the four south-east outlets which combined for a total percentage of 5.14. The north-west, where our expectations were initially low, surprised us with . . .'

Try to get the bad news out of the way first so you're not spending time working up to something they don't want to hear.

● **Topic Bridges**

Assuming that you're logically on target, with one topic following the other precisely where it should, you'll need devices for moving smoothly from one subject to the next. Here are several common transitions:

1 Reiterate the central theme: '*Computer security* in the workplace requires more than staff. It requires an attitude change.'

2 A personal anecdote: 'Three years ago, I had an experience with software theft firsthand.'

3 Summarize the points you've covered: 'We've seen how inattention to computer security affects management-employee relationships, research and development costs, and middle management morale. Now, we have arrived at the pivotal strain: the effects of computer crime on the individual office worker.'

4 Transitional phrases: Use short words or phrases to move from one subtopic to another:
   'Let's *sum up* the results of the survey.'
   '*However*, the story doesn't end there.'
   '*Continuing* with our discussion on target marketing . . .'
   '*Inevitably*, there are complications.'
   '*Thus far*, we've seen how . . .'

Non-verbal transitions include:
5 Pause: Take three seconds before continuing. When you resume speaking, your voice will signal another idea.

6 Use stage business to change topics: Take a sip of water, turn partly to another sector of the audience, shift eye contact etc.

7 Use body language to indicate a new subject: Shift your weight, change your gestures etc.

● **Vivid Examples**

You can support your main thesis with raw data and still be correct within the context of a business presentation. In fact, you're better with data than extraneous pyrotechnics.

Sometimes, however, the facts beg for colour. Instead of torturing yourself in a search for 'something to brighten it up', look back to the introduction and borrow a few attention-grabbing techniques. Anecdote, analogy, quotations and visuals are all applicable to the middle of the presentation, albeit a bit less flamboyantly. Pack your talk with colourful examples and don't be stingy about sharing your personal experiences. To save you the trouble of flipping pages, here are seven of the more useful attention-holding devices to use in the main body.

1 Quotations: 'Mark Twain said it all about being a boss in 1899 . . .'

2 The statistical chorus line: 'Due to malpractice insurance, we lose enough obstetricians a year to staff every inner city hospital in Dundee, Leeds, Birmingham, London and Cardiff.'

3 Provocative questions: 'Ask yourself if you would send your own son or daughter into our Beirut facility. You wouldn't, would you?'

4 Comparisons: 'Let me give you an example of how large that plant is. If you took the roof off, a Boeing 747 could land on the main assembly floor while another took off from a complete halt.'

5 Provocative statements: 'If I can find the time to process the paperwork, every member of my team will either jump out of a plane or walk across a bed of hot coals before the summer is out.'

6 Cite an authoritative source: 'Most of us, according to the *Wall Street Journal*, can expect to make major career changes three times before age forty.'

7 Recall your own experience: 'I've been fired, and I can tell you firsthand that it is not a pleasant experience. It is, however, a growth experience.'

Visual Eloquence

Since those awful traffic safety films in primary school, we've been conditioned to put our minds on overdrive when the lights dim for slides, tape or movies. Flipcharts, maps, transparencies and mounted photographs are usually received with all the enthusiasm of a magazine subscription circular.

Yet speakers persist in plugging holes with visuals. People aren't stupid. They know the difference between the enthusiastic use of a visual and using them to kill time. As fortification to a good presentation, visuals are a powerful tool and a serious option if you have to speak for more than ten minutes.

Here are five good reasons to use visuals:

1 They divert attention from you: Visuals fill out the stage or meeting room. There's more for the assembly to see.

2 Visuals reduce stage fright: They remove a lot of the pressure from the presentation. But that pressure, as we have pointed out, is energy. Anything that siphons nervousness from a talk also takes away the edge afforded by anxiety.

3 They clarify data: Three-dimensional computer graphics can make any set of facts look well thought out. The audience greatly appreciates being shown what the facts and figures really mean.

4 They increase interest in the topic

5 They increase the likelihood of retention: They may well forget your face or what you wore, but your listeners will always remember a good visual.

And here are four good reasons *never* to use visuals:

1 Because you have stagefright: Visuals help with stagefright, but they are too often used as a pill. For the non-phobic (most of us despite the liberal use of the term), the only real cure is gruelling, galley-slave rehearsal. Adding bells and whistles to your presentation to relieve anxiety is like taking a couple of drinks to deal with a problem. Sooner or later, it catches up.

2 To fill time: There's virtually no such thing as a well-prepared talk that runs too short. If your topic is tightly covered before the alloted time, too much time has been allotted. Deal with it another way.

3 Because you think there should be something besides you: Maybe there should be another panellist or an audience participation segment on the presentation instead of a visual. Maybe you should go it alone. In any event, the job of the visual is focused supplementary material, not flickering light because it's there.

4 Because you would rather be directing movies: Video is an ego thing, let's face it. Editing tape brings out our Spielberg fantasies. You could easily OD, lose your objectivity, and produce your way to boredom.

● **Using visuals effectively**

1 Never try to substitute them for yourself: You are the best visual in the room. The way you walk, dress, hold the room, and zero in for a one-to-one talk with the audience should be paramount in your planning. You can achieve dramatic results with pace, gesture, body language, demonstrations and vocal range. Use visuals sparingly to augment this natural leadership. Don't allow them to take over your act.

2 Consider objects before technology: A ball-bearing which killed a family of four, a fly in a beverage which resulted in a three-million-dollar settlement, and other objects which can be passed around a conference table, are often far more effective than a slide presentation, film or video.

3 Place visuals to accentuate your central theme: Many speakers fall in love with a visual only peripherally related to their main thesis, then try to stretch. What they really stretch is their credibility.

4 Keep everything large: Use upper case lettering, large numbers, projection video monitors if available, and elevated screens for films, slides and transparencies. Lines and drawings on charts should be bold and heavy.

5 Avoid
(a) Too much detail in a visual aid
(b) Blackboards, because they don't reflect light well and we all hate them anyway
(c) Crowding lettering.

6 Test everything ahead of time: That includes plugs which you've been assured work, flipcharts, transparencies, the angles of elevated visuals, and all equipment. When something goes wrong later, the only help you'll get from the hotel or conference centre staff is momentum-killing delay and lame excuses about its working yesterday.

7 Keep visuals out of your way, and invisible until you need them: If they're obtrusive, visuals impair your delivery. Keep them, if not out of sight altogether, to one side, below the lectern, or otherwise away from centre stage.

8 Talk to the audience not to the visual: When you're working with a screen visual, there is a strong temptation to shift towards it as you speak. Continue to address your audience once you've assured yourself that the apparatus is in place and functioning.

9 Don't stand in front of the visual

10 Don't allow the visual to block your audience's view of you

Slides, film, and video: tips for maximum impact

- **Slides**

The old slide show – a static series of still pictures punctuated by an annoying bell which told the operator to move on – has been replaced by dazzling multi-media extravaganzas with quadrophonic sound, three-dimensional imagery and other special effects. Automated speed control facilitates a smooth mesh of your pace with the equipment. Here are four good reasons for using slides:

1 They're flexible. You can adjust their use to last-minute changes.
2 They make spectacular use of colour, depth, and texture
3 They're portable
4 You can easily control their use as you speak

Now for the three main disadvantages:
1 They can make you look stupid. They are very accident-prone. The longest fifteen minutes of your life may be when you see a tray of slides fall off a table
2 They do not accommodate last minute graphic changes
3 Slides can, let's face it, be boring

● **Film**

One of the best things you can do with a good slide presentation is have it transferred to filmstrips. Then the operator just puts the cassette into the projector and rolls. Here are three advantages to using film in any form:

1 Film is beautiful
2 It is available from a thousand sources at little or no cost
3 Projectors, screens, and other hardware are usually available where you speak

Five disadvantages of film:
1 Film breaks
2 When films get old, they become scratchy, grainy, stretched and distorted – and they get old very fast
3 The subject may fit, but the film is often outdated enough to wreck your credibility. Always preview personally any film you plan to show

4 Films get the jitters
5 Projector operators lie a lot about what they know

● **Video**

Video has lived up to its long-trumpeted promise as a revolutionary corporate information-processing vehicle. In the past five years, three-quarter-inch industrial cassettes (the large ones you can't use at home) have replaced film in most sizable AV departments.

You probably have a seasoned video producer down the hall. You may never have paid attention to this person because he or she looks far too young to be of any help. Like computers, video has attracted a lot of bright youngsters who know their field thoroughly before they're old enough to buy a legal drink.

Industrial video, like its home counterpart in the half-inch format, was prohibitively expensive until recently. Ten years ago, a five minute talking-head production would have cost £15,000 or more. Today, you can get the same job done, in house or outside, for less than a thousand.

Here are some tips for working with video:

1 Use it for training: If you slip up, you can erase and shoot again. Any situation where employees or management need to see themselves is ideal for video.

2 Learn to edit before you need the knowledge: Video is edited electronically on a computerized deck. The setting is usually you and an editor who lines up the visual image for each shot. Then it's a take or it isn't. Video editing is a long process much like putting a puzzle together. You have to have the larger production constantly in your mind. The worst time to learn editing is under the pressure of a deadline.

3 Shoot far more footage than you need: Most of your raw footage will be unusable for a thousand reasons. Since you've got the crew there, keep them busy shooting a lot of tape. You'll thank them later.

4 Have raw footage logged: Someone (and you're way too busy yourself) has to sit down and note where everything is on every cassette. Never go to an editing session without such a log.

5 Never shoot industrial footage on a home recorder: The unit is of inferior quality to a three-quarter-inch machine, but the real problem is lighting and cameras. Home VCRs will make the boss look like a featured player in 'Night Of The Living Dead'. You won't be forgiven.

6 Make sure you shoot lots of close-ups: You'll need them later for editing. Don't assume that the crew will remember to shoot these cutaways on their own.

7 Hire a producer-director with experience in your field: You can only find out how good someone is by word of mouth. Ask to see the producer's demonstration reel and make sure there's something on it that relates to your situation.

8 Take full charge of your production: There's a lot of commotion as people you've hired push you out of the way. Don't let them. When they're done and gone, you have to answer for any mistakes they've made.

The disadvantages of videos are:

1 They are not easily integrated: A video breaks up your act. Sometimes that can be good but, if you're on a roll, you forfeit your momentum.

2 We're accustomed to high professional standards: In corporate video, we aren't able to compete with network budgets and talent. Our video timing and pace often leave audiences vaguely dissatisfied.

3 We often overlook audio: Only recently have video producers started to focus on solid audio production. Many production people, brilliant in putting together the video patchwork, mess up the sound. Meshing sound with picture is a very important skill. Don't overlook it.

4 Video is tops in production excesses: A good production facility has so many special effects (cubes, rolling characters, 3-D, fast zooms, slow zooms, dancing numbers) that their use is a constant temptation. Special effects are cream puffs to a dieter. A sure sign of amateurism is reliance on such devices.

5 They're frequently too long: A minute in video is a very long time. Even fifteen seconds on one shot is so long it's painful.

6 The monitors usually aren't very good: Television monitors often have a dusty, fuzzy, quality from improper maintenance.

Flipcharts, storyboards, display panels, photographs and other non-electronic aids

Non-electronic aids never short out and, unless they topple, rarely interrupt the flow of your presentation. A flipchart is probably the most user-friendly device in the world; go forward, backward, hold the visual as long as you want, and it will be there for you. Here are a few tips on using the basic visuals.

1 Let them do the talking: If the storyboard shows a man walking into an office building, you don't have to tell the audience that they're looking at a man walking into an office building. Be subtle.

2 Use static visuals only in meetings/small group discussions: They just won't work if your audience numbers more than twenty-five to thirty.

3 Use a pointer: Your index finger won't do.

4 Never turn your back to the audience: Static visuals lure you into turning from your listeners. Stand with your face to the audience and turn slightly to the side as you point out your key displays.

5 Keep everything large: Keep your printing so large that you feel like a first-grade teacher.

6 The visual can't be too crowded

7 Be careful if you're transporting charts or cards on public transport: If you're moving the flipcharts or storyboards by car, you're in good shape. But if you try putting them on an airliner or a bus you'll see that you need another type of visual. They just don't travel well.

Instant Review

There are five good reasons to use visuals:
1   They divert attention from you
2   They reduce stage fright
3   They clarify data
4   They increase interest in the topic
5   They increase the likelihood of retention

Four good reasons not to use visuals are:
1   Because you have stagefright
2   To fill time
3   Because you think there should be something besides
    you on stage
4   Because you like directing movies

Using visuals effectively
1   Never use them as a substitute for yourself
2   Consider objects as visuals before going hi-tech
3   Use them only if they enhance your dominant theme
4   Keep everything large
5   Avoid too much detail, blackboards and crowded
     lettering and characters
6   Test everything ahead of time
7   Keep visuals out of sight until you need them
8   Talk to the audience, not to the visual
9   Don't stand in front of it
10   Don't allow it to block you

Slides
Are flexible, colourful, portable, and easily integrated. They
can also make you look bad, can't accommodate last-minute
graphic changes, and can be very boring.

Video
The state of the AV art for the rest of the decade and beyond;
learn to use it before you need it; shoot and log more footage
than you need; shoot lots of close-ups; take full charge of your
production.

Words with Clout

Most of us stop developing our language skills far too early, which is unfortunate, because success and verbal skills are inseparable. You will find the occasional folk hero who never got beyond the eighth grade and went on to earn millions, or the athlete replete with double negatives, but they are rare. Successful people usually convey precision and force when they speak.

Watch a good CEO in a meeting. His text is spare and packed with information. You won't need a dictionary to understand what you are told. It is never the jargon-laden sludge of the specialist. That's for middle management. It is not full of imagery and rich phraseology. That's too vague. There are no long detours to spare feelings. The point is right out front, and usually attached to some action. You can almost tap it with a pencil and hear its clarity ring out.

Expanding your language ability doesn't mean reading the dictionary to absorb big words. More often, it means reducing those polysyllables like verbal fractions. You already know how. If you're a college graduate, you recognize about 60,000 words, as many as in the whole English language of Shakespeare's day. Write for the ear. Homer was a singer, Shakespeare an actor. Mark Twain swatted big words like so many flies and made a pretty good living without them. You will too.

• The Magic Monosyllable

The most forceful words in our language are monosyllabic: God, love, fight, hate, help, hurt. The most provocative emotion you can convey is packaged in a four-letter word. When you bang your thumb with a hammer, what word comes right out? If you get cut off by some jerk at an intersection and nearly lose your front end, do you want to *discuss* the matter? The right word is there in a syllable.

Leaders have known this for centuries:

'I have a dream' (Martin Luther King);

'Give us the tools and we will do the job' (Churchill);
'Ask not what your country can do for you . . .' (Kennedy).
We fight and die with monosyllabic inspiration:

> Keep America free
> Loose lips sink ships
> Remember Pearl Harbour
> War is hell
> Buy bonds
> The war to end all wars

In corporate life, you can apply the magic monosyllable to many of your daily communications problems:

Conciliatory gestures
'I'm sure we can work it out.'
'I know we'll come to terms.'
'When we get together, we do it right.'

Hardball
'I don't think you heard me right. I don't want your help, I want to make a deal. You know it, I know it. We deal, or we come in and stomp on you.'

Gratitude
'I don't know how you get your work done, but you always do it well.'
'Your help meant everything to the job.'

Here are six additional high impact language strategies:

1 Imprint your position with a personal stand: Show your belief in what you say by coming forward and putting yourself on the line:
Low Impact: 'Many in the company want to see a re-evaluation.'
High Impact: 'I say we re-evaluate.'
Low Impact: 'It could be argued that there are other solutions.'
High Impact: 'My reaction is that there are other ways to look at it, and I'll tell you what they are.'

2 Euphemisms are low impact: 'Members of minority groups might object.'
Instead say:
'Black people won't like it at all.'
'Their financial assets are dwindling.'
Instead say:
'They're running out of money.'

3 Use absolute words and phrases: Adding 'all' to a phrase frequently strengthens it.
Low Impact: 'Our employees are factory-trained.'
High Impact: 'All our employees are factory-trained.'
'Should' carries clout: 'You should get it done fast.' But 'really should' is low impact: 'You really should get it done fast.'

4 Abbreviations are low impact: 'The EAEC, the ECU, and the MRE are cooperating with the USN in its investigation.'

Spell it out: 'The European Atomic Energy Community, the European Currency Unit, and the Microbiological Research Establishment are cooperating with the United States Navy in its investigation.'

Remember that jargon is low impact unless everyone uses the terminology every day. Even then, think twice before using it in a presentation.

5 Use the active voice:
Passive (low impact) voice: 'The referendum will be voted upon by the executive council.'
Active (high impact) voice: 'The executive council will take a vote on the referendum.'

6 Use softeners sparingly: In a meeting, where power often flows from chair to chair, diplomacy might call for padding your position with a softener, such as, 'It seems to me that . . .' In a presentation, you should deliver an equivocation-free communication. That leaves out hundreds of insurance phrases in the English language. Here are some of those power pollutants:
'I could be mistaken but . . .'
'I'll double-check my facts, but . . .'
'Is it me or did I observe . . .'

'I don't want to appear sexist . . .'
'I know that you might interpret this as . . .'
'It seems to me that . . .'
'Time may prove me wrong, of course, but . . .'
'I am fully aware that the law prohibits theft of software, but . . .'
'In my opinion . . .'
'It is the judgement of many, including myself, that . . .'

Here are ten of the worst phrases you can use:

1 I know we all face an important challenge
2 We will conquer the future with teamwork and optimism
3 We welcome the opportunity to prove ourselves in the face of adversity
4 The future is ours for the taking
5 Let us rise to the occasion and pull together
6 I don't see problems, only opportunities
7 There is no goal we cannot reach when we put our heads together and forge ahead
8 The challenge of tomorrow starts today
9 We are a people company
10 The whole is far more than the sum of its parts.

Business presentations are so filled with challenge, teamwork and optimism about the future that they have no bite. Such structural clichés mean nothing to the speaker or the audience. Remember our need for emotional nourishment. Hit them where they live.

• Tripartite division

Philosophers, then linguists and behavioural scientists, have long observed the mind's craving for breaking things into three parts. Don't buck the system. Whatever your message, there are three parts to it. If there weren't before you started writing the speech, there are now: 'The solution is three-fold.' 'The programme has three principal components.'

We carry tripartite division as happily as six-packs on Cup

Final day. Always attach organizational emphasis to this system. But just because everything *can* be broken into three components, you're not required to do so.

● Use contrast

'I am forced every month to *lie* to the accounting department in order to get reimbursed for an *honest* business lunch with a colleague.'

'I would rather be a *champion* production manager than a *mediocre* vice-president of manufacturing.'

'There was once *sloth*, now there is *ambition*. There was once *discontent*, now there is *harmony*. There was once *anger*, now there is *joy*. There was once *apathy*. Now there is *pride*.'

● Repeat for emphasis

'There are three things to remember about retailing. Location, L-o-c-a-t-i-o-n, and LOCATION!'

● Don't explain in a presentation

You never owe anyone an explanation for being at the front of the room as in: 'Let me explain how I came to be here this afternoon,' *or* 'My getting to this point is a long story, but I'll shorten it as best I can,' *or* 'I can explain why the agenda has been changed. Just give me a minute.'

● Use Financial Shorthand in Meetings.

'They want 30K more than we're willing to spend, but I'd rather eat it than blow a 16 mil deal.'

Warning: Don't use it in formal speeches.

● Adjectives and adverbs usually dilute

This is not to say they aren't useful, but there are often alternatives:

'I got to the plant on a *dark* and *stormy* night.' All nights are dark. Stormy could be a lot of rain, drizzle, hail, sleet, or snow. To clarify:

'It took me until midnight to get through three feet of snow to the plant.'

Adverbs – really, actually, frankly, sadly, happily – have a place, but not a big place. They too should be used sparingly.

● Nurturing words are weak

The Sensitive Seventies are long gone and so is all the talk of business with a moral mission. Not that you have to get up there and act like you're personally kicking Khaddafi in the groin as you speak, but words and phrases such as 'sensitivity', 'human potential', 'getting in touch with . . .', 'reassure', 'feed', 'nurture', 'non-threatening', and 'feelings' carry a connotation of public-sector babble.

● Diminutives insult

A 'nice little facility', or a 'sharp little operation' won't score you any points with your audience.

● Phrases With Too Many Words

Low Impact	High Impact
In point of fact	Nothing or in fact
A total of	Just give the number
To be perfectly honest/candid/ frank	Nothing; what were you before?
To tell you the truth	Skip it
As a matter of fact	In fact, or delete
Under the present circumstances	At present
When you check into the facts . . .	When you look closely
Be that as it may	But
Long in duration	Long
Suffice it to say . . .	Delete
At the present time	Now
As you are aware . . .	Delete unless you're saving some dolt embarrassment

As you may already know	You may have heard
Advance planning	Plans, Planning
Are in agreement with	Agree
At this point in time	Now
Due to the fact that	Because
Oddly enough	Oddly
Is fully operational	Works well
In view of the fact that	Because
In close proximity to	Near
Predicated upon	Based on
Close personal friend	Friend
With regard to	Regarding
Thusly . . .	Thus . . .
Irregardless of . . .	No such word; try irrespective
Of sufficient magnitude	Big enough
Until such time as	Until
Impact on	Effect
At the present time	Now
Right Now	Now
Consensus of opinion	Agreement
In view of the fact that	Although
A highly personalized account	A personal story
She relates well to	She relates to
So great	Great
The body of work	The work
In regards to	Regarding
An ongoing programme	A programme
For all practical purposes	Delete
For all intents and purposes	Delete
Yours is a point well-taken	Good point
In the event of	If
End result	Result
Each and every one	Each
In the course of	During
Different than	Different (or different from)
Give credence to	Believe
For the purpose of	For
New innovation	Innovation
Never before and never since	Never

The Conclusion: Your Big Finish

The conclusion is your final opportunity to leave an impression. It has to be big. Fortunately, the finale is far easier to prepare than the introduction. It says nothing new, it is always brief, and it carries the bonus of elevated audience attention. There are four goals to a conclusion:

1 The tip-off: You have to tell them you're ending to cash in on the increased energy always present at the end of a talk. Even the weakest tip-off, 'In conclusion', snaps people awake. More muscular ones include: To summarize, Let me leave you with, Finally, Summing up, Before I finish, I'd like to, As we part company, I'll end with . . .

2 A quick summary of your main points: We do mean quick. There's no faster way to nullify a great talk than to promise the end and not deliver.

3 A parting shot: Give them your most vivid story, quote or personal experience to blend your purpose in speaking with your central theme. A parting shot might be: a personal anecdote, a call to action, a rhetorical question, an inspirational hammerlock, a short piece of humour or a quotation.

4 A final salutation: Don't just say 'Thank you' or 'Thank you very much'. Look right at them and thank them for the dinner, the hotel suite, the pleasant stay in Dublin, or the courtesy extended. Limit this salutation to a single sentence, but personalize it.

● **The four musts of a conclusion**

1 It is always very short

2 The language must be muscular, as in: 'We won't ask anyone's permission to be in this market. We'll get them out of our way.'

3 It must be realistic: If you call your audience to action, ask them to do something uncomplicated: 'Vote. That is all we ask,' or, 'I want you to do two things: give a pound and ask a friend to give a pound.'

4 It must convey promise: Even when the news is bad, there should be some direct focus on a time when things will be better.

Remember that a conclusion should also refer back to the introduction and tie up the package:

'Returning again to Socrates . . . he also said . . .'

'I went back to that mattress factory and found Oscar still at the machine twenty-five years later.'

'When I began, I said there were four reasons to purchase gold this year. Let me add a fifth . . .'

- **The must-nots of a conclusion**

1 It must not introduce a new topic: Tell them what you told them, give them a goodbye kiss in the form of your parting shot, and you're out of there. Don't say anything they haven't heard.

2 It must not be confusing: That summary is just a tit-bit, a headline from your main body. Don't make it complicated.

3 It must not apologize: The conclusion is no different from the introduction in this way. If you're bombing, go down gracefully. Don't tell them you wish you had more time or that they should have seen you yesterday in Amsterdam.

4 It must not be shrill or preachy: They'll get the idea if you want them to do something. Don't scold them for 'falling down on the job' or some such damnation.

5 It must not be condescending: Looking down on someone, even in what might be considered a nice way, is really the pits. If you have power, show it non-verbally, but be watchful of being such a 'regular guy' that you invoke hostility.

Instant Review

The conclusion has to be big. With it, you seek to do four things:
1 Tip off your ending
2 Summarize your main points
3 Give them a parting shot: a personal anecdote, a call to action, a rhetorical question, an inspirational hammerlock, a quotation, or a short piece of humour
4 A final salutation

The four musts of a conclusion are:
1 They are always short
2 The language must be muscular
3 A call for action must be realistic
4 You must convey promise

The five must-nots:
1 Don't introduce a new topic
2 Don't confuse anyone; summarize briefly
3 Don't apologize
4 Don't be shrill or preachy
5 Don't condescend

Section II: Deliver!

This section hands you the keys to that Porsche. If you follow its guidance, you can climb right in, gun it and create a special place for yourself in the corporate structure.

People who can deliver a good presentation don't wait around long for the breaks. Senior management sees to it that the right doors open quickly. As your presentations improve, you'll see that people treat you differently.

First, you have to pick up a few tricks about speaking authoritatively from notes. The High Impact speaker never hides behind a text. Powervoicing is next. You'll learn to turn your voice into an instrument of authority and conviction. You'll find out the quick way to get rid of those annoying mannerisms, like 'Uh', 'Uhm', 'Y'know' and other Low Impact impediments. Your voice will work for you instead of against you.

The body language of meetings and presentations comes next. For thousands of years, we've used non-verbal language to tell people what we think. You'll be able to fashion your body language to hammer your words home.

You won't find a chapter on overcoming stagefright. The High Impact system calls for as much nervousness as you can find. The more nervous you are, the better your presentation will be. 'Just Before You Speak' (pp. 86–9) ignores the usual platitudes about preparation being the best medicine, or of picturing your audience naked to take the nervousness out of the moment. For a business presentation, you need straightforward techniques to convert stagefright into High Impact speaking power. You have them.

Knowing 'The Cycle of the Presentation' (pp. 92–3) helps you with something show people know about and business people rarely learn – timing. By understanding when the audience is with you and what you can expect from them at various times in your speech, you turn the odds in your favour. You will be able to put your shots where they will do the most good.

'Sounding Like You Mean It,' (pp. 104–6) offers the strategies you need for putting everything together to form a memorable delivery.

Claiming the Room When You Speak from Notes

They won't trust you if they don't have your eye contact. Business audiences need to look you over, check your validity, and make decisions as you speak. You can't have the luxury of reading from a prepared text, which is good because a script puts up a Berlin Wall between you and the people you're supposed to be convincing. All great speakers give the illusion of extemporaneous speech. You can learn their tricks if you follow a few basic rules.

Remember to prioritize your meetings. If you give a meeting an A, approach it with an emotional black tie or formal gown. It's a biggie and major talks have to be put through the phases and rehearsed fully.

A high-priority meeting or formal speech

1 **Draft the talk to your specifications of completeness:** For most of us, this means a typed text with complete sentences and paragraphs. You might be more comfortable abbreviating such formality, but you should be thorough.

2 **Read the talk through from the draft several times:** Practise rolling the words around, pausing, projecting to the back of the room, raising your voice, lowering it to a rumble. Have fun, but move on quickly.

3 Develop a rehearsal outline: Your rehearsal outline should be pretty fleshy. Leave in the introduction and conclusion in their complete form. Key transitional phrases, quotes and other statements which require precision should also be left. The rest, however, should not be in sentence form, such as:
– Stagflation not gone, just gone out of language
– Non-productive activity burdens a third of our technical professionals
– The so-called 'sunrise' industries aren't rising
– R&D undernourished

4 Develop a spare topical outline: Now, even the word-for-word intro and conclusion are gone. Don't let your hefty rehearsal outline become a security blanket. Once you get up to speak, it's useless in that form. Be brutal in getting rid of notes until you have only the seven or eight main topics of your presentation, quotes and data.

NO STRONG RECOVERY

CAPITAL DIVERTED: 1983 deficit hit 69.4 billion, increased by 100 per cent over next two years
STOCKPILE OF WEAPONS NO LONGER NATIONAL SECURITY CAN PROVIDE FOR NATIONAL DEFENCE WITHOUT IMPAIRING ECONOMY

A low-priority meeting

Sometimes we have to look good for only a few minutes in a meeting whose agenda applies primarily to another department or division. There's no time to draft a fancy introduction. In these meetings, there's no way even to know if you'll have to speak. Here's what to do:

1 Be prepared with points you consider important and relevant

2 Craft them into short punchy sentences: Put the data on index cards and slip them into your pocket. Think through the sentences, writing them out until they're sharp. This takes no more than five minutes.

3 As you glance at your data card, shoot the sentences out as though they had just occurred to you: Just let them flow. If the occasion for their use doesn't come up, they will be useful in another meeting. Keep a supply of these punchy statements tucked away. They often take less than ninety seconds to prepare and you'll always find a use for them.

Remember that a high-priority presentation requires about a dozen run-throughs. Even a low-priority remark which is to appear spontaneous should be voiced a few times at home.

Instant Review

High priority
1 You need eye contact for credibility
2 Make a very thorough draft
3 Read through from the draft several times
4 Develop a rehearsal outline
5 Develop a spare topical outline

Low priority
1 Be prepared with one or two points you consider important and relevant
2 Craft them into short, punchy sentences
3 Let the sentences flow as though they just occurred to you
4 If you don't use the remarks, file the cards away

Using Body Language to Show You're in Charge

The next time you have to be near a hospital, watch the doctors. You can spot one across a car park long before you see a name plate, stethoscope or surgical scrubs. Doctors rule their profession and everyone gets out of their way. They walk and gesture in concert with their status. Even the way they push the elevator button says, 'I am a doctor and I earned it.'

Tape a television drama on your VCR. Watch it with the

volume down and see if you can figure out what's going on. Turn the volume up and you'll find you were probably accurate, for body language never lies.

Modern studies of non-verbal communication date not from the talk shows of the early seventies but from the Victorian era, when Darwin noted that all species with limbs cross arms when they perceive a threat. Don't take his word for it. Point your finger at someone's face and, if you don't get slugged, you'll see a half-dozen gestures of closure.

Common sense is the watchword in interpreting signals. If an associate likes what she's hearing, you'll see the openness reflected in the gesture. Arms will extend, she'll lean forward, nod and tell you with her eye contact that whatever you're selling, she's buying. If you're not being well-received, you'll soon see a drawing back, constriction and turning away. Body language is a part of most chapters in this section, because it is integral to any discussion of one-to-one and small-group communication. Before we look at the basics, here are some truisms to remember.

1 Mixed signals are not uncommon: Body language has at least a 50,000-year evolutionary jump on the spoken word. It is always a complex series of cues, some of which may be contradictory, especially when a person is making a decision.

2 Sell yourself on your material before concentrating on body language: Actors always look for the core of the character they play. They know they must immerse themselves in the motivational roots of any role to be convincing. If they have not found them, your non-verbal radar picks it up. They can't fake body language; it has to flow naturally. So we are back at the old High Impact adage of believing in your presentation or argument. Movement for its own sake is futile.

3 High Impact body language is always deliberate: People in control have an expansive, space-garnering way of walking. Their heads are high, the pace is no-nonsense, and the demeanour says, 'I have a deadline.'

67

4 Jerky, uneven movement is Low Impact: Those with little chance of claiming a room move in uneven, fidgety spurts which beg to be interrupted. There is a halfway effort at one gesture, followed by another small move, then another. They never seem relaxed.

5 High Impact speakers complete their gestures: You never have to wonder if a speaker is in control. You know by his gestures. A hand move sweeps right up and punctuates a point. It completes its cycle.

6 The High Impact pace is brisk but relaxed: You're always going somewhere and the room knows it. Your pace is soothing to them because they know you're at the controls. However, you are never, never hurried. Hurried is Low Impact.

7 Your eyes set the pace: Your eyes are the key in body language. The rest of your gestures should merely confirm your eye message. If it is off, the rest of the body language won't help you much.

8 Never try to monitor body language when you give a formal presentation: This is in the category of never monitoring your own performance as you speak. You'll get vertigo and fall. There is plenty of time for body language study during the informal discussions that follow. Body language monitoring is for meetings only.

9 The High Impact speaker's body language is as spare as his text: A leader never has to overstate the case. This fact of corporate life is as true in gesture as it is with the spoken word.

10 Answer assault with forward movement in meetings: We've mentioned the pointed finger, which is one of the most hostile gestures one human can make to another. If you get that index finger, don't show a sign of retreat. Move forward, invading your attacker's space and keep your face expressionless.

Body language for a presentation

1 Stand with even weight on both feet: Plant them right in cement when you take over the front of the room. Don't shift weight.

2 As you deliver, move your body towards various parts of the room: Most people try to connect with the audience simply by moving their heads. It's not enough. Go all the way. Move your body three or four times as you face various sections of the room.

3 In long talks, walking is permissible: You can move around a bit if you're on stage, but you shouldn't dart or do it too often. Pacing, usually done in little steps, is very Low Impact. A space-grabbing, deliberate walk to the front of the podium, especially during key changes in pace, is High Impact.

4 Hand gestures should be complete, and downward: Practise gesturing by making your right hand come up and then firmly down when you make a point. Then, switch to your left hand. Up, then firmly down. When practising, do this once or twice every sentence. After much practice, the large, firm gesture becomes a strong, unconscious asset. Remember to orchestrate with only one hand until you're far along. Even then, two hands gesturing at the same time usually have all the impact of a pair of windscreen wipers.

5 Don't use the lectern as a support: You can anchor yourself by touching both sides of the podium when you start, but real impact comes when your hands are not holding it as a crutch.

6 Walk to your position like a millionaire in his grounds: Be sure to check it out ahead of time, so you don't stumble and blow the whole effect. When you get there, pause. Take five seconds or more to look directly into the faces of your audience.

Eye contact

Good eye contact with your audience is not merely an imperative in a business speech. It is your ticket to credibility. You should use your eyes to underscore your points, to challenge, amuse and drive home your main points with the explosive crackle of a jackhammer.

An old speaking adage holds that you should look just above

the heads of the audience to avoid the intimidation of direct contact. No way. This is akin to learning to type with your thumbs. You'll get good only when you learn to make a crisp, compelling connection with your audience through eye contact. Look directly at them except for brief breaks when you can refer to your topic outline. Say hello to someone on the left with eyes that blaze with conviction. Feel the snap of rapport, move down or to the right and say hello to someone else for a second.

● **Eye contact in a platform speech**

1 During the pause before your intro, make your first eye contact: Don't just meet someone's gaze – communicate. Your face should be honest, open and unafraid of a smile. It all starts with your eyes.

2 As you deliver, move from the far left to the near right in a Z pattern: Any movement from left to right is fine, but remember that you have to connect with the front, middle and back of the audience.

3 Don't feel you have to stop at every face: Since you are elevated, the face you choose to greet with your eyes represents everyone in his or her sector of the audience.

4 Don't stare: Eye contact is not a duel in the prison yard. Just say hello and move on after a couple of seconds.

● **Eye contact in a meeting**

1 Make sure you can be seen: Regardless of the pecking order, find ground where you can stand up and present your ideas to everyone in the room.

2 Get yourself up to higher ground: If you have enough material for a few minutes, stand up. Don't apologize, even if it does represent a departure from company sociology. No one faults a speaker who stands and takes over. If you're bound by the informal executive style of senior management, or have so little time to speak that getting up would be awkward, sit up straight and lean forward.

3 At a table, make gradual eye contact: A horseshoe or oval conference table nullifies the possibility of systematic eye contact with your audience. You can, however, get where you're going by moving across the terrain in an unhurried, but definite, manner. Eventually, you'll look everyone's way and fulfil the eye contact requirement.

Body language in meetings

When sitting through someone's presentation:
1 Show respect by keeping both feet on the floor. Don't cross your legs or ankles, and don't sprawl.
2 Your lower back should be flush against the chair
3 Keep your hands visible and still
4 Use your eyes to show interest in the material

You send signals of discomfort or nervousness if you
1 Tug at your clothes
2 Play with an object such as a pen
3 Tap your feet
4 Jingle change in your pockets
5 Scan the room to assess the reaction of others
6 Drum your fingers on the table
7 Cover your eyes and peep through your fingers
8 Run your fingers through your hair

● **Reading body language during meetings**

Remember, if you're presenting, don't try to read body language. It is a dangerous self-evaluative measure which will impair your delivery. But, in the give-and-take of most meetings, you increase your odds of getting what you want if you can read the gestures of others.

These are 'yes' gestures:
– Open hands
– uncrossed arms or legs

- several rapid nods
  (not constantly nodding)
- chin stroking
- steepling of hands
- leaning forward
- a slight touch in a one-to-one meeting
- the head tilted towards you.

These say 'no':
- Crossed arms, legs, ankles
- clenched or tightly-folded hands
- buttoning a jacket
- tilting the head away from you
- putting an object between you as a shield (straddling a chair, holding out a pen, holding up a clipboard etc)
- showing you any piece of the back (some executives tilt around, turn their heads away, or pointedly face away from you)
- hands that cover the mouth
- holding the back of the neck with the palm
- looking down
- scratching the head (or running fingers through hair)
- lacing the fingers of both hands and stretching them towards you

While this chapter is not meant to substitute for a more comprehensive book or course in body language, it should provide you with a few thumbnail reference points to get you through your business day.

Instant Review

Body language
1 Watch doctors at a hospital, or television with the sound off, to observe how body language works
2 Mixed signals are not uncommon
3 Sell yourself on your idea before concerning yourself with any aspect of body language
4 Body language is unhurried and deliberate if you want to project a High Impact image
5 Jerky, uneven movement is Low Impact
6 Complete your gestures; don't go halfway
7 Be brisk, but relaxed
8 Your eyes set the body language pace
9 Never try to monitor body language as you speak to a group
10 Be as spare with your body language as you are with your text
11 In meetings, answer assault body language with forward motion

In presentations
1 Stand with even weight on both feet
2 As you deliver, move your whole body as you face various segments of the room
3 In long talks, a little walking about is permissible
4 Hand gestures should be complete and downward
5 Don't white knuckle the lectern
6 Walk to your speaking position like a millionaire in his grounds

Eye contact in a platform speech
1 Look directly at the audience, not somewhere above their heads
2 Make eye contact from the far left to the near right
3 You don't have to connect with every face
4 Don't stare at anyone

In a meeting
1 Present where people can see you
2 Make gradual, not abrupt, eye contact if you're at a table

Body language in someone else's presentation
1 Both feet on the floor; don't cross anything
2 Your lower back should make contact with the back of the chair
3 Hands visible and still
4 Show respect by giving your speaker eye contact

Don't
1 Tug at your clothes
2 Play with an object
3 Tap your feet
4 Jingle change
5 Scan the room to see what others are doing
6 Drum your fingers
7 Cover your eyes
8 Run your fingers through your hair

'Yes' body language
– Open hands
– uncrossed arms or legs
– several rapid nods
– steepling of hands
– stroking the chin
– leaning forward
– a slight touch
– head tilted towards you

'No' body language
– Crossed arms, ankles, legs
– clenched hands
– buttoning jacket
– tilting head away
– turning around or showing you any piece of the back
– shielding
– covering the mouth with the hands

- looking down
- scratching the head
- lacing the fingers of both hands and stretching in your
  direction
- holding the back of the neck with the palm

Body language is a complex system of non-verbal
communication. Read a book or take a course for a more
comprehensive view.

Powervoicing

The voice is the great untapped power resource of business
communication. With very little practice, you can use it to get
what you want. You can, at will, apply vocal subtlety to
seduction, persuasion, intimidation, consolation, desperation,
extreme confidence – and expect to achieve your goals. People
automatically judge you and make decisions on your education,
socio-economic status, and seriousness of purpose by the sound
you project.

Few of us ever bother to tap this subconscious oil well. We're
not lazy, just intimidated. Nature gives, nature takes. One of her
sick jokes is housing our vocal apparatus next to the inner ear.
We hear a much nicer voice than we project. It is fuller, more
resonant, and more precise in conveying the emotions we want
to transmit. That braying ass on the tape is someone else.

The speaking pattern you put across is an attic filled with
jagged pieces, long-forgotten gadgets, and uneven piles of your
life. There's a little bit of elementary school here, the army
there, a camp counsellor who once made an impression, and the
five years you spent in Newport as a child. You have an accent,
or a combination of accents. The way you talk is a learned
response, and what can be learned can easily be re-learned.

The speech therapist is probably the last bargain of the health care field. The people in this profession are miracle workers who can show you a thousand opportunities for voice improvement. Your ear, nose and throat specialist probably works with several, or you can usually find a speech clinic at a large university.

Do not try to change the following yourself:

1 Stuttering
2 A heavy regional accent
3 Lisps, muffled consonant sounds (such as the L) and other articulation disorders
4 Physical problems such as harelips or conditions resulting from injury
5 Hoarseness, severe nasality, excessive stridency of speech and other advanced problems

But here are the components of speech you can improve with as little as five minutes practice a day:

1 Voice quality: You can make your voice clearer, free of distraction, and in control.

2 Pitch: People believe a lower pitch. Women sometimes say that this luxury is yet another unfair benefit of being male. They are not wrong, but they do leave a lot of possibilities untapped.

3 Volume

4 Breath control

5 Speech mannerisms: Maybe someone told you that you smack your lips or make some other distracting vocal sound when you want to underscore a point. Or you fill space with 'Uh', 'Uhm', 'Like', 'You know', 'Well'. It will take a while, but you can clean up this clutter yourself.

6 Ryhthm is where you emphasize words, stop for air, place your pauses, and how you time your delivery. It is probably the most pliable element of your speech. If you work on it, you'll change your rhythm radically.

7 Speed: Nervousness produces an accelerated wavering pace. Speaking too slowly also diminishes you.

● **Getting ready to work on your voice**

1 Tape yourself in everyday speaking situations: Keep a cassette near the dinner table and record your conversation. Enlist the help of your partner and tape a conversation, or record your half of a phone call.

2 Evaluate your strengths: It is time to get beyond the 'Oh, I hate the way I sound' phase and move on to a positive evaluation of your speaking strengths. Focus on what's good and work towards fortifying these.

3 Work on one problem at a time: If you want to improve pitch, work only on that. If you try to do too much, you'll probably quit.

4 Allocate little time, but keep to a schedule: Five minutes a day is plenty when you keep a busy schedule, but it should be five minutes *every* day. It's the only way you can realistically expect to improve.

5 Don't be the perfectionist: perfectionism is one of the great ways to get nothing done. If you've worked five minutes a day for two weeks, getting rid of an 'uh' mannerism, you'll see exhilarating improvement but not perfection. Improvement should be enough.

6 Problems always return: When the baritone voice-over announcer gets tired, traces of his upbringing – his attic – return to his speech pattern. You might get rid of an accent, talk to your mother on the phone, and find it's returned. This is no big deal. Just keep working at it.

Now, here are tips for improving your use of the voice as a power tool:

● **Vocal quality**

1 Run your index finger down your windpipe to your larynx, that small protrusion you may know as an 'Adam's apple'. Feel

it as you speak a single syllable. It should be even, like the steady buzz of an electric razor.

2 If there is 'noise' in the form of gravel, or other uneven qualities, you will feel the larynx ride up as you speak.

3 Take a deep breath, swallow and make a prolonged vowel sound: 'Aaaaaaaaaaaaa'.

4 Tense your voice, you will feel the larynx rise again, and the noise will return.

5 Practise alternating the less tense, less noisy sound with the harshness.

● For minor breathiness

If you can hear the wind rush through your speech, sending exuberant or seductive signals where they do not belong:

1 Slow down your pace
2 Breathe only between natural segments of the talk
3 Practise inhaling and exhaling silently.

A little breathiness is a plus. Too much distorts. Speech therapists are especially good with this problem, which may be medically based.

● Pitch

To lower the pitch of your voice:

1 Open your mouth wider when you speak: Your mouth is a natural resonating chamber, which, when opened, brings your voice level down to a more convincing pitch.

2 Practise by alternating your normal pitch with a lower level:
(a) With the tape recorder running, say 'Aaaaaaaahhhhhh' in your normal speaking voice.
(b) Loosen up by taking three slow, deep breaths, then rolling your head around its socket comfortably.
(c) Now, open your mouth much wider and say, 'Aaaaa-aahhhhh' again. You'll hear the difference and your tape will confirm it.

(d) Keep alternating tones; first, use your regular pitch, then open your mouth and hold a note on a deeper pitch.

3 Read aloud at the lower pitch

4 Finally, try it in conversation on a limited basis: Eventually, your pitch will be more authoritative in conversation. Remember not to expect miracles. You've been speaking at the same pitch since you were a child, and you're not about to burst on the scene suddenly as some kind of conference room Pavarotti. Work slowly.

● **Volume**

Powervoicing is not being loud. Very often, it's lowering your voice, so those around you have to lean forward to hear. A few tips:

1 Practise projecting to the far corners of various rooms: Get someone to stand at the end of the room and throw your voice directly to that person without changing pitch. Try a small room first, then a larger room. You'll find that you shout and distort at first, but that is only a temporary condition. The overmodulation will soon be replaced by an even, controlled level which will serve you well in meetings.

2 Work on lowering your voice: When you are away from the office, experiment with variations in volume; lower your voice to make a point and watch as friends move towards you. Increase your level to your normal volume range and lower it again.

3 Watch the pros: Look at television with a new perspective, and observe how talk show guests and comedians use volume for emphasis and timing.

The powerful person talks at an even volume, feeling free to summon higher or lower voice range when needed, but sparingly. People who talk too loudly display the insecurity of someone afraid of being interrupted. If you're too soft-spoken, people will walk right over you. Speak at an even level, and be calculated about your use of the highs and lows.

- **Breath control**

Your voice rides on a column of air and is tapped into speech as it comes through your mouth. The air column rests on a foundation known as the diaphragm, the home base of power-voicing. You can find it by placing your palm just below the rib cage, and above the navel. To speak from the diaphragm, you must first assess your posture.

Standing for a presentation
1 Stand on both feet, with your legs shoulder width apart. Your body weight should be evenly distributed.
2 Keep your head raised to the eye level of someone your height, so that facing each other you both make eye contact.
3 Your chest is raised, and your stomach tucked in. This is not to say that you have to scrunch in a paunch. That's another exercise altogether. You're not covering your midriff, just bringing it to some kind of attention.

Sitting for a meeting
1 Sit up straight. Most of us touch the back of the chair with the upper torso, when the lower back should be making the contact.
2 Place both feet on the floor and leave them there. Don't kick off one shoe, cross your legs or sprawl while you're speaking. You probably shouldn't do any of these things anyway but, when you speak, it's both feet flat.
3 Place your hands together, but don't lock them. You'll need them for gesturing.

Tapping the diaphragm's power
To reach way down for your speaking energy, and reap the benefits of the diaphragm's natural control, take four steps:
1 Inhale and, with your palm, see if your abdominal air sucks in or presses out. It should press out.
2 If you exhale steadily, forcing air out at an even pace, you will make direct contact with your diaphragm. Practise counting as you exhale, and increase the count with each exhalation.
3 After exhaling, and forcing out as much air as you can handle, inhale again. Make sure your abdominal muscles move *away* from the body.

4 When you have practised several steady inhalations and exhalations, open your mouth wider than usual and say a few words. You will feel the power of diaphragmatic speech.

These four steps soon become part of your unconscious speaking pattern; you won't have to think about them.

• How to fix speech mannerisms

Speech mannerisms are nervous conversational habits such as 'uh', 'uhm', 'You know', and 'Like'. They can also be non-verbal sounds such as an involuntary giggle, clearing your throat or smacking your lips after every question.

The hardest part about kicking mannerisms is pinpointing them. We simply don't notice them. Assuming you can identify one, here are four tips for getting rid of it:

1 Write it on an index card and carry the card with you. If you have an 'uh' mannerism, write 'uh' on a card by itself. Look at it two or three times a day.

2 Tape your conversations. Keep a cassette recorder near the phone or in some spot where you can reach over easily and turn it on as you talk. Let it run at various times for a few days before playing back your conversations. This will show you the extent of your difficulties with the mannerism.

Be accurate. If you normally say a contracted 'Y'know', don't bellow out a clear 'You know'.

3 Read the newspaper aloud, interjecting your mannerism as you go along. Be brutal. Do an exact impression of yourself. Work from a minute to five minutes each day at this. Don't overdo it, or try to remake your speaking life in a few lengthy sessions.

4 If you've done other vocal exercises in this program, you're becoming familiar with an alternating practice of correct and incorrect. This method is known as *successive approximation*. It means, keep moving towards a goal and you'll get there. Successive approximation works well with mannerisms:

'I, y'know, want to, y'know, go to Bristol and, y'know, visit the branch office, y'know.'

'I want to go to Bristol and visit the branch office.'

'I, y'know, want to, y'know, go to Bristol and, y'know, visit the branch office, y'know.'

'I want to go to Bristol and visit the branch office.'

Successive approximation takes the mannerism from the unconscious to the conscious where you can see and conquer it. Think of a mannerism as a bug that bites you, then disappears before you can find it. One magic moment, you've got it and ZAP!

● **Rhythm**

'I love the idea.'

There's a simple sentence that meets the High Impact criterion of monosyllabic clout. It is a sentence with no hidden agenda. How would you say it?

'I *love* the idea.'

If you emphasize 'love', you put your commitment on the line. Your listener will never get paranoid. But, suppose you said the same words another way:

'*I* love the idea.'

Now your listener won't sleep. If *you* love the idea, who doesn't? The big boss must hate it. The executive committee wants someone's head for thinking up such porridge on company time.

'I love the *idea*,' or worse, 'I love the id*ea*.'

Such emphasis indicates something incomplete. Sure, kid, the id*ea*'s fine, but you left out anything more substantial.

Most of us spend our lives paying no attention to the flow of our conversation. To orators like Winston Churchill, Martin Luther King, John F. Kennedy, Billy Graham, leaving rhythm to chance was unthinkable. If Lyndon Johnson had paid more attention to his advisers and got a speech coach, he might have served another four years, for his public speaking rhythm was one of the few things the man never mastered. Picture how low the impact if Dr King had said, '*I* have a dream.'

● **Pauses**

You can pause almost anywhere in a presentation and pull it off if you take your beat deliberately:

'Never come through that door *again*!' (Pause)
'*Never* . . . come through that door again!'
'Never *come through* . . . that door again!'
'Never come through *that* door again!'

But a pause should only be long enough to establish your emphasis, usually 1–3 seconds. Too long or too much pausing in a talk, is Low Impact.

It doesn't matter where you take your pauses, but **take them so you mean them**. The speech rhythm of an effective speaker is the pace of a Jaguar on the M1 – sometimes a little faster, sometimes just a hair too slow, but never uneven, always smooth and deliberate.

● **Speed**

There is no correct speaking speed, but if you're beyond 160 words per minute, you're too fast. If you crawl at 110 words a minute, you need speech training.

People in control are never in a hurry. They generally go a degree below normal and appear to use words carefully. They don't shift gears. Jerkiness signals lack of control. Practise as you do with pitch. Slow down and watch as they anticipate, speed up and they'll get a message of urgency. Avoid extremes either way. Enunciate clearly. Don't run words together as you try to get your point across.

● **Punching up your voice**

Once you're on a roll improving isolated problems, put it into the context of your new vitality. What else needs to be done? Practise reading aloud and underlining newspaper words for volume. Then underline groups of words for pauses and emphasis. Draw slash marks where pauses occur:
'The first thing the company president noticed was that his room had no windows.'
'The *first* thing the company president noticed/ was that his room/ had no *windows*.'

Actors and announcers follow this practice and use the notes as a roadmap for producing the sound they want from a piece of copy. If you practise with a newspaper or magazine, you'll learn the secret of professionals; eventually you'll automatically head for the optimum use – the High Impact configuration – of your voice.

Instant Review

Your voice is probably your least utilized source of presentation power.
Your vocal rhythm is an attic filled with scraps of your whole life
What can be learned, can be unlearned

Work with a speech therapist on:
1. Stuttering
2. A heavy regional accent
3. Lisps, muffled consonant sound, articulation disorders
4. Physical problems
5. Hoarseness

But you can improve:
1. Vocal quality
   (a) Take a deep breath, swallow, and make a prolonged vowel sound
   (b) Tense your voice, forcing air through it unevenly
   (c) Alternate 'noisy' and 'clear' pattern

2. Pitch
   (a) Lower your voice by opening your mouth wider
   (b) Loosen up with deep breaths
   (c) Reach way down for a prolonged vowel sound
   (d) Alternate with the shallower vowel sound of your regular speaking voice

3. Volume
   (a) Powervoicing is not being loud. Often it's being softer
   (b) Too loud is insecure
   (c) Practise projecting your voice to the furthest corner of the room
   (d) Watch the pros and how they use volume

4. Breath control
   (a) Keep diaphragmatic speech as your goal
   (b) Develop strong posture
   (c) Practise tapping the power of the diaphragm

5 Mannerisms
  (a) Harder to identify than get rid of
  (b) Write mannerism on a single index card and refer to it
  (c) Put mannerism into your conversation deliberately
  (d) Read the paper aloud, injecting mannerisms
  (e) Alternate mannerism and mannerism-free speech for practice

6 Rhythm
  (a) You can influence your effect by the deliberate emphasis on words or syllables
  (b) Use pauses carefully, only to separate groups of words, and never too long. Take dramatic pauses deliberately
  (c) Speech rhythm of a person in control is always deliberate

7 Speed
  (a) There's no right or wrong speed
  (b) Monitor yourself and decide where you are
  (c) Avoid extremes
  (d) Enunciate clearly: don't run words together

8 Punching up your voice
  (a) Practise reading aloud and underlining words for volume
  (b) Underline groups of words for pauses and emphasis
  (c) Use slashes to separate phrases and indicate a pause
  (d) Eventually, you'll underscore your main points automatically

Just Before You Speak

Is there anything more absurd than trying to relax before a presentation? Forget that nonsense. If your body is pumping adrenaline to every remote corner, your legs feel they're about to give way, your mouth is a dry lake bed, and you can clean the coffee table with your palms, your emotions are in place. You're ready to kick butt and use that energy to turn lacklustre into blockbuster.

The following techniques won't relax you, but they will help you put adrenaline to work on your behalf:

1 Don't try to fight your physiology. Own it. Stand still for a moment and feel the physical manifestation of nerves: shoulders, legs, neck, chills, weakened knees, stomach flutter. These vibrating sensations won't get out of control once you allow them to flow through you.

2 Focus on a single object for thirty seconds while breathing deeply. It might be a glass or a spoon, a pencil, anything in the room. Concentrate on every inch of that object as you breathe deeply. You'll be amazed at how much power you feel.

3 Place the fist of one hand into the palm of the other and push on each end for ten seconds.

4 Plain old deep, slow breathing is a great control mechanism that goes all the way back to Socrates' time. Breathing alone, however, is way too passive. It needs focus. When you inhale, think 'Iiiiiiiin' and when you exhale, it's 'Ouuuuuuuuuuuuut.'

5 Crumple a napkin or a piece of paper into the fist of your hand, squeezing as hard as you can until the count of five.

6 Rub your hands together rapidly (when no one is around, of course) focusing completely on the build-up of heat and energy. As you do this think clearly about the positive aspects of your talk and visualize a successful result.

7 Take a deep, slow breath as you extend your arms outward as far as you can. Stretch and repeat the exercise a few times.

8 Clench both fists tightly and punch downward with one hand, then the other. This will loosen you up considerably.

9 Tilt your head to the left, stretch, and return to your normal position. Now stretch to the right and repeat the motion until you're feeling in control.

10 Visualize a gauge with your energy level on a 1–10 scale.

Take stock of where you feel you are at this minute, then raise the level a couple of notches.

11 There are thousands of de-stressing possibilities and most of them focus on a simple cycle of tensing, then relaxing your body's muscles. If you can get into the habit of putting a few of these physiological tricks to work just before an important presentation, you'll become a much better speaker.

12 Don't rely on alcohol or drugs: Let's face some truth here. A chemical hit, be it a prescription drug, a controlled substance, or a shot of booze *will* remove inhibitions. That's why people use them. But no drug works as well the second or third time out and, as you well know, you eventually find the dosage going up as your effectiveness goes down. Learn the reality early; the more clearheaded you are, the better you are. Take it easy on even the coffee.

There is a prescription drug called propranolol that appears to block stagefright. It is non-addictive and not a tranquillizer. But it is a drug and all drugs have a price. See your doctor if you need it, but don't need it.

Instant Review

1 Don't try to relax. Choose a few de-stressing techniques and get into the habit of working out just before a talk
2 Focus on a single object, breathe deeply
3 Place the fist of one hand into the palm of the other and push
4 Plain old deep, slow breathing is still a great trick but focus as you breathe
5 Crumple a napkin or a piece of paper into your fist and squeeze
6 Rub your hands together rapidly
7 Take a deep, slow breath as you extend your arms outward a few times
8 Clench both fists tightly and punch downward with one hand, then the other
9 Tilt your head to the left, then to the right, and stretch
10 Visualize a gauge with your energy level on it and raise it a notch
11 Experiment with tension/release until you develop the de-stressers that work for you
12 No alcohol, no drugs

Claiming the Room in the First Thirty Seconds

Whether you're addressing eight people in a conference room or a thousand conventioneers, the room is usually yours if you seize it in the first half-minute of your presentation. The audience wants you to be good, and they're willing to give you the chance, but they want something very expensive in return. They expect you to take over.

Encouraging though it may be to think that a good speaker can get anyone, they're not always within your reach. It could be a hot afternoon and they've been listening to dull talks for three days. The only thing between them and a cool drink by the pool is you. You'll never beat those odds.

People who put conferences together, bless their hearts, are a little short on timing and showmanship. You could be scheduled behind the keynote speaker who has been flown in from Washington and paid ten thousand dollars because of his fame and ability to leave audiences in tears, begging for more, which he just did. Now, it's your turn.

Aside from such dramatic, but all too common, exceptions, however, the first thirty seconds of a talk is yours. Depending on the size and mood of the audience, you may even have up to five minutes to fortify your authority, but you must establish control at the top of the talk. Here is how you do it:

1 Develop a confident walk: When you're in public, you're an actor, so act. Even though your innards are feeling like a bowl of uncooled jelly, stand tall and walk directly to the podium. Don't try to move too quickly. Remember your body language.

The walk is an overlooked, yet critical, piece of non-verbal communication that gives your audience its first view, and judgement, of you. If you strut out there like a rooster entering a barnyard, then stumble through the introduction, you'll almost be able to hear the sense of letdown. You sent mixed signals, and you're already not delivering. If you shuffle diffidently, you are telling them you don't deserve their attention. And you won't get it. Walk purposefully.

2 The actor's mask: Actors and actresses train themselves to assume the look of the characters they portray. You too have to put on a face. Your eyes must sparkle with focus as you walk to your speaking position. Your face has to insist on their attention without trying too hard.

Find your most pleasant and assured facial demeanour and mentally pull it on as a mask. If you try this old stage trick, you'll find the mask slippery at first, but eventually you will almost feel the right look click into place. Once you have it, it will always be there.

3 Plant your feet in cement: A tip-off to insecurity is erratic movement of the hands or feet. If you fidget, you may be a podium dancer who shifts from foot to foot, or taps around the lectern in constant motion. As bad as this is on stage, in a conference room it's a straight-out disaster. They'll scarcely hear a word you say.

To help anchor yourself, picture placing your feet in two buckets of wet cement which then solidifies and holds you there. You don't have to stay in the cement forever. We've pointed out that moving a bit, and turning your whole torso to face the audience is High Impact. For the introduction, and the early part of the main body, however, you should consider yourself planted right into the floor.

4 Touch, but do not grasp, the podium: If you are giving a platform speech, you may touch either side of the podium for an instant of anchoring leverage. Don't hold both sides as you speak, and don't cling to the wood like it's a lifeboat and you just jumped from the *Titanic*.

5 Pause: Once you are in place, you'll be tempted to take off like a gazelle. Pause instead. You'll find pauses throughout your talk to be very calming. Make eye contact with your audience to ascertain that they won't eat you. Now take a deep breath. Put your notes exactly where you want them.

When you have followed these steps, the pause before you begin is almost beatific. Instead of terror, there is calm. You've yet to say a word, but you know you've got it. Your mask is in place, your hands and feet are where they're supposed to be. You know the introduction and conclusion as well as your phone number, and you can move through the main body with only a glance at key phrases from your topic outline. You actually get excited when you think of the powervoiced delivery ahead of you, backed by the body language of your enthusiasm and conviction.

You are ready. At this moment, you understand why public people love their work. During this flash of a pause, you realize that the podium or big meeting is not a death sentence, but opening night or home ground. It is showtime, your opportunity to do something spectacular.

Begin your talk.

Instant Review

1. Develop a confident walk
2. Put on your actor's mask
3. Plant your feet in cement
4. Anchor yourself by touching the podium
5. Pause
6. Take a deep breath
7. Begin to speak

The Cycle of the Presentation

The audience follows a predictable path through any delivery. Knowing its cycle will help you mesh your content with the ebb and flow of attention. Here are guidelines:

1 Strong or weak, they'll be there for your introduction: The audience will sniff you out and weigh your message against its collective needs. This is why audience analysis is so important. If you don't have anything new or applicable to their experience, they'll tune out.

2 Write some of them off for the main body: They just won't be there. It might be their problem, it might be yours, but you will lose a piece of your crowd once you get into the substantial, but unpizazzy, main body of your presentation.

3 A diehard group will be with you through even the quietest moment: As surely as Perry Como's fans wouldn't celebrate Christmas without one of his prime-time specials, you too have a core of supporters who will age with you through the presentation. Don't worry about finding them. You'll naturally meet them as you make eye contact with the audience. They will give you strength.

4 Visuals wake everyone up: Plan their use at natural lulls in your presentation. With them, you can buy time you might not have without visual aids. But visuals only wake the audience up if they're used sparingly.

5 A new topic creates a stir: Never be shy about telling them you're into something new. Different members of the audience will come with you on certain topics, while others will take a break. Don't worry about this phenomenon. You're no different when you're a listener.

6 If they buy you, they'll laugh at your humour: An audience doesn't really laugh at a speaker *per se*. They laugh when they buy the speaker's *persona* and feel a consensus of approval from fellow audience members. No one wants to be the only one laughing.

7 A pause brings them alive: Use the built-in expectancy of pauses to regroup and win them back. So long as you're not overdoing it, they'll follow you.

8 When you signal your conclusion, there's a jolt of alertness: Now the whole family is back. You've told them you're ending, and they feel they owe you a final burst of attention. This is where you pour it on and finish big.

Instant Review

1 They'll always be there for your introduction
2 You can write a portion of your listeners off as soon as you get into the main body
3 Conversely, a group will be with you no matter how tough the sledding
4 Visuals, strategically placed, wake everyone up
5 A clear indication of a new topic creates a stir
6 If they buy you, they'll laugh at your jokes
7 A pause brings them alive every time
8 When you signal your conclusion, there's a jolt of alertness. Finish big.

The Q&A

A question and answer session follows virtually every presentation you give. Be cool, concise, and follow these steps:

1 Recharge between the end of your talk and the Q&A: Too many Q&As go down the tubes because the speaker is too relaxed to field sharp questions. When your presentation is over, enjoy the afterglow of being off the stove for a few minutes. Then, get yourself charged again because, though it's another form of public speaking, you're still on.

2 'I don't know' is a valid answer: If the question falls within the parameters of a well-prepared talk and you're not equipped to provide an answer, so what? Tell them you don't know.

3 Follow 'I don't know' with action and a timetable: While not knowing the answer immediately is valid, leaving it that way is never enough:
'I wouldn't hazard a guess on something so important, but if you leave me your card, I'll get you the answer by the end of the week.'

or

'Give me a few days after I return to Newport. I'll call you Monday with the answer.'

Of course, if it's an area only tangentially related to your field, you owe the questioner nothing. Still, it is High Impact to make, and keep, a promise:
'That area isn't even remotely related to what I do, but a friend of mine knows the field well. If you leave me a card, I'll have her call you.'

4 Watch for two or three questions posing as one: This is one of the all-time, world class, Q&A blunders. You hear two or three questions and you try to answer them in a few sentences:
Say: 'I'm hearing two questions here. The first is about toxic waste. The second is about regulation. I can address the waste.'

5 No debates: There's always some clown who misses college bull sessions and wants to start one at your presentation. Allow a question, then a follow-up to be courteous. Then say: 'I think this is getting too involved. I'd be delighted to discuss it with you when we're through.'

The debater will probably come to you afterwards but, without the audience, he or she won't be that interested.

6 Listen for text and subtext: Pay attention to notes of sarcasm, levity or other emotions lurking between the words of the question. If the intent is to embarrass or draw attention away from you, be polite and brisk. Sometimes subtext indicates curiosity the questioner can't even find. That's fine. Help him out by asking: 'I think I'm hearing curiosity about how we really get along back in London. Is that correct?'

7 Repeat the question when you hear it: Obviously a meeting of six people won't warrant repeating the question, but doing so usually helps people at the back of a room to become more involved with what's going on. Repeating the question also clarifies the issue.

8 If in doubt, ask if your answer is satisfactory: As in: 'Have I answered your question, Miss Partridge?'

9 Never dismiss the questioner: Assume that there's no such thing as a stupid question or questioner. Privately, you may have your doubts, but, if people are interested enough to ask, be flattered and provide a direct answer.

10 Don't be flippant: Flippancy is hostile and rude. It says you're more interested in what *you* have to say than the trivia of the questioner.

11 Answer briefly: No tangents or war stories during the Q&A, please. If it can't be answered in a minute or two, tell the person to see you after the session.

Instant Review

1   Charge up – a Q&A is still public speaking
2   'I don't know' is a valid answer
3   Follow 'I don't know' with action and a timetable
4   Watch for two or three questions posing as one
5   No debates
6   Listen for text and subtext
7   Repeat the question when you hear it
8   If you're in doubt, ask if you've answered the question
9   Never dismiss the questioner
10 Don't be flippant
11 Answer briefly

Persuasion

Persuasion is getting people to agree to your terms. In a broad sense, every trick in this book has been about persuasion. You talk people into things with all aspects of your presentation, from the way you walk through the door to how you fold your hands.

This chapter is the cognac of persuasion, the final link to a convincing message. When you have a meeting which ranks at the top of your priority system, use these techniques to get your way.

● Beforehand

1 Know your party: If it's a big meeting it's worth your time to look your principals up in *The Directory of Directors*, *Kelly's Business Directory*, *Kompass*, *Burke's Peerage* or *Debrett's Peerage*, *Who's Who in Business*, and *Who Owns Whom*. They're going to be written about somewhere, and one of your most valuable efforts is to learn about the people you wish to persuade.

2 Know the corporation: Company Annual Reports, *Economist* and other business publications are readily available. If a company does not belong to some trade association, you've probably found a family video store which hasn't got around to joining yet. Everyone is part of a larger group and that larger group has a publication. Take your time. Time is cheap in this case.

3 Ask around: Someone you're meeting is a golfer. A second is a horse freak. Another loves polar bears. A few calls to friends and associates often produce valuable information.

4 Store the knowledge: Those who gather information on the persuasion target often overplay. Be cool. It will probably be more useful to you if you never disclose that you took the trouble to find things out.

5 Form a link before you get there: Banks hate to deal with people their principals don't know. Since you can't meet every banker, or doctor, lawyer or car mechanic, you can form a preliminary networking link:

'I understand you're meeting tomorrow with Tom Lashnits.'
'Yeah, right. You know Tom?'
'He's a good friend of mine.'

You have a much better reception already. You don't have to have a friend make a call if it seems inappropriate to do so. You can just as easily drop a name at the meeting, or take some small step to form a bond. You'll find it's not a small step at all.

● **At the meeting**

1 Define its purpose right away: If you're there to interest them in your company, say so right off. You'll save a lot of time and possibly trouble, which could spring from a misunderstanding.

2 Ask the person you're meeting to define his or her purpose: Or, if you're meeting with a group, ask the principal to define the meeting. You have immediate feedback.

3 Location is up to the person you want to persuade: This is one of the great chicken/egg debates of persuasion. Some say you can be more persuasive on your own turf. Some say, the persuadee is more receptive on her ground. Chances are, you'll end up on someone else's turf if you want something from that person.

It's going well if
1 The body language is open
2 There's a lot of thoughtful nodding
3 Your opinion is solicited
4 Interruptions, such as phone calls, are curtailed or minimized
5 The leader of the group sends glances to the next person in the pecking order
6 Your sales materials and other supplements are solicited and passed around
7 A higher authority not at the meeting is mentioned or consulted.

It's not going well if
1 The body language is closed, withdrawn
2 There are constant interruptions
3 You get a tentative 'I'll have to get back to you on that', or a very qualified 'Yes'. A skimpy 'yes' is probably a way to get you out of there

When you hear 'no'
1 Ask for the problems immediately
2 Ask for an additional meeting if the problems can be dealt with
3 See if there's a new person who can be brought into the process
4 Tactfully determine the avenue of appeal; it's usually there
5 Find out, any way you can, if you are dealing with the right people

If it's still 'no'
1 Treat the 'no' as respectfully as a 'yes'
2 Allow a respectable, but minimal, time to pass
3 Come back with a revised proposal
4 Try to alter the cast of decision-makers
   If you're courteous and professional, persistence will never be

regarded as a nuisance. Corporations cannot handle persistence. They'll eventually give in to you.

Showtime: Running Your Own Meeting

The Eloquent Executive runs a meeting with the same blend of grace, technique and preparation that he or she brings to a platform speech. Not all meetings, of course, carry the same clout. For those which count a lot, and even those which aren't such a big deal, here are the steps when it's your turn to drive:

● **Before the event**

1 Decide if a meeting is necessary: Maybe you really need a head-to-head confrontation, an impromptu visit, or even a memo. If the occasion doesn't call for a formal sit-down, why add yet another to your life?

2 Decide who should attend: Use sound judgement based on protocol and need to know. The fewer people in most meetings, the better.

3 Review the playing fields: The meeting site is normally dictated by the available facilities. Most corporations have a 'big' conference room, and a 'small' meeting room, each with particular flavour and significance. Off-site meetings carry their own message, as does a gathering in your office.

4 Prepare your message: Remember the language of the ear and how stilted written words sound when spoken. Remember short words and phrases as you write out your text, then translate it to notes. Or, if there is no time or priority for an A presentation, go directly to the notes. Just know where you're going if you expect your audience to go with you.

5 Set an agenda and stick to it: If possible, have the agenda distributed twenty-four hours before the meeting. If you have a reputation as digression-prone, surprise them and hang in with a tight agenda.

6 Time your agenda by segment: If it's an hour meeting, divide the segments and the topics into four main pieces, and plan to be merciless about moving on.

7 Trim the agenda to the time limit: If there are more things to discuss than can be accomplished, take the excess out. Don't squeeze things in.

8 Check the scheduling of the meeting: Monday at nine isn't great. Friday at four is even worse. If there's a marketing meeting every Wednesday at ten, setting a Wednesday session to begin right after lunch won't win you any friends. People have to anchor themselves between meetings.

9 No hidden agendas: Corporations are Kremlinesque enough. Don't have people wondering what this is really all about. Be up front. Remember the natural paranoia of the people you invite. If you inadvertently leave someone out, he or she may feel a sense of danger.

● **During the meeting**

1 All speaking rules apply: There's no band, no rubber chicken, and no Sunday dress in your meeting, but you still have to claim the room right away and hold it. If you're developing cobwebs, check the Instant Review on the area that gives you trouble.

2 Summarize as you progress: If it's an hour meeting and you've divided the agenda into four parts, recap every fifteen minutes and move on.

3 Build in discussion time: If people can't discuss their ideas, even in a straight informational presentation, it's not a meeting. It's the army.

4 Don't allow time-consuming conflicts: Those little turf battles will eat up your time and waste energy every time. Stomp on them before the meeting and, when they inevitably surface, firmly tell the warring parties to focus on the agenda and schedule another meeting for their problems.

5 Appoint a facilitator to keep you on course: More managers are turning to a neutral facilitator appointed at the beginning of the meeting, or before, to keep things on course. This person is usually respected by all factions, or has no aura of threat. His or her job is to make sure the gathering doesn't disintegrate into a pillow fight. But if you appoint such a person, abide by their judgement. Otherwise, the judge can't give out sentences.

6 Impose firm rules at the outset: If Rambo wants to wave his bayonet, give him two minutes, not three. Or three minutes, not four. Make people summarize what's been said before rendering judgement on a point. Be an iron parent, because it's the only way you'll keep control.

7 Encourage full participation: Save yourself the hassle of the person who says little at the meeting coming up to you afterwards with a detailed outline for a plan. Ask people for their opinions.

8 Start on time, end on time: Let those who come late and leave early read the minutes. Develop the reputation of punctuality. In some environments, you'll take a bit of peer teasing. Even then, it will be a good-natured poke. Punctuality always reflects professionalism and control.

9 Be tactful and ask polite questions: Don't turn your meeting into a hockey game or allow others to do so.

10 Re-direct questions: Don't answer every question yourself, just because you are in charge. Encourage full participation by taking a question from one group member and asking another to comment on it: 'Sarah, you worked that territory for three years. What do you think we should do?'

11 Finish big: Your presentation may be broken up by the give-and-take of a meeting, but you still need that big finish. End with a spirit of accomplishment.

12 Build in follow-up: Never leave with a general 'We'll have to do something about this' attitude. If you took up an hour or more of company time, you should have resolved something specific. Build in follow-up, someone to do the tasks, someone to check on who did them, and when they will get done.

● **After the meeting**

1 Evaluate its productivity: This can take the form of a few minutes with a colleague on the way back to your offices, or thirty seconds with yourself. But don't just let it sit there. Ask if it was worth the time, if it was adequately prepared, if the agenda was sound, if the follow-up reflects the substance.

2 Put it in writing: Get those minutes out right away, properly copied to senior people. When some clown who said, 'Hey, yeah, I'll get to it' reads he's going to have *gotten* to it by Tuesday, that's religion!

3 Track down the follow-up: Others may just fill air to sound good, but be an executive who gets results. That happens when everything gets done when it is supposed to be finished. Make the excuse-givers look as weak as they are. When someone has a valid reason for lack of follow-up, be patient – once. Without action, you've just burned up time and money. You might as well have gone out for a walk.

Instant Review

Before the meeting
1   Decide if the meeting is necessary
2   Decide who should attend
3   Review the possible settings for it
4   Prepare your message well
5   Set an agenda and stick to it
6   Time your agenda by segment
7   Trim it to meet the time limit
8   Check the scheduling of the meeting
9   No hidden agendas

During the meeting
1   All rules of good speaking apply
2   Summarize as you progress
3   Build in discussion time
4   Don't allow time-consuming internal conflicts
5   Appoint a facilitator to keep you on course
6   Impose firm rules
7   Encourage full participation
8   Start on time, end on time
9   Be tactful and ask polite questions
10 Redirect questions
11 Finish big, as usual
12 Build follow-up into your meeting

After the meeting
1   Evaluate productivity, however briefly
2   Put it in writing
3   Follow-up on the follow-up

Sounding Like You Mean It: Strategies for Effective Delivery

1 Know your introduction and conclusion cold: No matter how much time you have to steal, get the intro and finale down so tight you know them better than your children's names. When you do, you are assured of two strengths:
(a) You're guaranteed to start well.
(b) You have a parachute for bailing out any time you want.
  If it isn't going well, you can just plug right into that conclusion and be out of there.

2 Sell yourself on the material: You can't pretend interest, enthusiasm and commitment. You have to believe in what you're saying. If you don't, speak another time. Personal enthusiasm is the magic pill that transcends voice, timing, pace and all other aspects of delivery. It is the only element which has to be perfect; the rest can be flawed.

3 Never try to evaluate your performance as you speak: When you try to gauge how you're doing, you put a big scar on your talk. You become nervous and tentative, and more so as the audience responds to your insecurity.

4 Be yourself: You can tap into a secret, more public, dynamic side of your temperament. That's fun. But don't try to become another character, or you'll fall flat.

5 Don't videotape yourself with a home unit: This is probably the only speech programme where you will receive such advice, but I maintain that you will weaken your presentation if you tape your rehearsal on a home VCR. The lighting is straight from 'Night Of The Living Dead'. The tape has probably been used a hundred times, and the colour is usually awful.
  All these shortcomings could be dealt with but for the human trait of brutal self-judgement. We murder our self-esteem when we see ourselves on camera. Even the best equipment adds

pounds, but a home recorder can distort so badly you'll think you're seeing yourself in an amusement park mirror.

If you want to treat yourself to the many advantages of a video, find a small studio and work out. It will cost you a bit, but they'll coach you. They will also transfer the work tape to VHS and you can watch it at home all you want.

6 Keep your body language lean and mean: Pages 66–75 tell you a few tricks.

7 Rehearse, rehearse, rehearse: Bear in mind that turning phrases over from notes as you travel or commute is valid rehearsal. Focusing word for word on the intro or conclusion are also rehearsal sessions. Give at least a half dozen complete runthroughs of a major talk, and more if you can steal the time.

8 Choose your wardrobe carefully: Some prefer brand-new outfits for major presentations, while many feel that new clothes have not adjusted to the contours of the body. Set aside early what you like and don't waste time on the day trying to put an outfit together. Wear your speaking clothes when you rehearse. Actors and actresses don't go through the dress rehearsal ritual because they love it. It helps them snap into their roles.

9 Visualize a successful speech: Always form a strong mental image of the meeting room or auditorium and picture the audience receiving you warmly. Work on this image as you rehearse and you will be surprised at how close to reality strong visualization can seem.

10 Don't fight nervousness: Anxiety is almost invisible to the audience under normal speaking circumstances. But let it creep in and take over and your whole character is perceived as uncertain. Preparation and enthusiasm are enough to succeed.

Instant Review

1   Know your introduction and conclusion cold
2   Sell yourself on the material
3   Never try to evaluate your performance as you speak
4   Be yourself
5   Don't videotape yourself on a home unit
6   Your body language must be as strong as your text
7   Rehearse a lot
8   Choose your speaking wardrobe carefully
9   Visualize a successful speech
10 Don't fight nervousness

Section III: One-to-One

Much of our speaking takes place in small meetings, sometimes with only a single individual present. If we're asked to give a *speech*, we prepare, fret, worry, feel awful, feel wonderful, have a drink afterwards, and forget the whole thing until next time.

However, an impromptu meeting, a business lunch, a conference room soccer game with a tough cast and your head as the ball, or a simple cocktail party are also, in a sense, presentations requiring strategies and preparation. Everything you know about an 'audience' as a collective group assembled to watch you speak applies here, with the addition of specific strategies which will help you to cope.

This section offers you the tools to look confident and apply all the principles of sound communication in a one-to-one environment. Sometimes it's easier to be effective before a thousand people as you make believe you're talking to a single individual, than to prepare, stand tall and execute your presentation to that one person.

Fortunately, one-to-one communications problems are usually remedied more quickly than those we face when we address larger groups. More often than not, these problems lie with our tendency to relax too much. Who has to prepare so much for an impromptu meeting or some lunch? Hell, shouldn't you just be yourself? Maybe, but look around. How many of your colleagues did themselves in because they gave a bad speech? Some, yes. But now count the number of people you've seen go down because they decided to wing it at the wrong meeting, lunch, or cocktail party.

Head-to-head requires a lot of thought and, sometimes, more preparation than any speech you'll ever give.

Head-to-Head: Effective Presentation to an Individual

Many of your most important, and career-building, meetings take place as you present your ideas to one individual. It might be an important client, or your direct supervisor. Their outcome often determines your future for many years.

Unfortunately, such meetings are often overlooked because we think of 'speaking' as standing on a stage and talking to people we'll never see again. The following tips, combined with other High Impact techniques, will strengthen your head-to-head skills.

1 Arrive unencumbered: If it's raining, get rid of your raincoat and umbrella. Leave them in the reception area – anything not relevant to the meeting should not be visible.

2 If you go into someone's office, make that person come towards you: Or at least meet you halfway. Don't be eager to sprint across the room and kiss a ring. Don't throw the power balance to the person you're visiting.

3 Give a firm handshake: As you shake your meeting partner's hand, pull slightly towards you, giving a businesslike grip. If possible, let the other person break the grip first.

4 Be equal: While it will always be clear if your partner has more corporate power than you, or more financial clout, there is never a reason to convey less than equality. Acknowledge your companion's official superiority while making it clear that you own your own life.

5 Be respectful: Sometimes it's hard to find anything to respect in the jerks we meet every day, but failure to acknowledge the person's worth is one of the principal reasons one-to-one meetings go down the tubes. Whether you're head-to-head with a superior or subordinate, being respectful is imperative.

6 Replace 'I' with 'you' whenever possible: You should conduct a one-to-one meeting with an approach to your partner's attitudinal base. Beware of lapses into the first person singular. Being 'you' oriented is an overall attitude which will achieve rapport, even where you didn't think it possible.

7 Treat your partner as an audience: It is clearly difficult to take a one-to-one meeting as seriously as a speaking assignment. The temptation to wing it is strong, and that's fine. You can't go into every head-to-head meeting as if it were the United Nations, but when it's an important one, you need even more preparation than a speech. Your language has to be careful and vivid, your confidence absolute.

8 Think tall: Stand tall, walk tall, sit tall, and talk with the tall person's ease. Height has little to do with this technique. Just be as tall as you can. Your whole *persona* will change.

9 Don't enter the room talking: Walk directly and quietly towards the person you're meeting, and extend your hand. If you go in talking, you show nervousness and uncertainty.

10 Turn your whole body squarely to your partner: Don't use only your head. Your whole body squared directly to the person greeting you signals confidence, control and a sense of inviolable turf.

11 Clear your hands before the handshake: Though it's not always possible, anything you can do to rid yourself of luggage – brief-case, raincoat, or other encumbrances – before the handshake strengthens your impact. Put it on the chair where you intend to sit.

● **Getting your message across eloquently**

1 Get right to the point: A few preliminary social observations, and go right for it; get to the purpose of your message.

2 Always ask: 'what would be in it for me if I were this person?'

3 Check for understanding: Language is interpreted in different ways by different people. As you go through the presentation, take understanding breaks and ask, for example: 'To summarize where we are, June, you want to see better cooperation between our departments, you find my assistant arrogant to yours, and you're unhappy about the timetable. Is that what I'm hearing, so far?'

4 Nail the meeting down with concrete follow up action: Never leave a head-to-head meeting with a vague, 'I'll get back to you', if you have the authority to set a timetable for follow-up action. Even if it's got to be somewhat unresolved, you can still get back to the person Thursday morning sometime after ten and before noon. You'll be twenty times more effective when you follow-up.

- **To get information**

Sometimes, the purpose of your meeting is to get information from someone. Here are tips to do so:

1 Establish rapport immediately: Coercive techniques are usually unnecessary and ineffective. If you're looking for specific information, your best approach is to establish common ground right away. You can do this indirectly with a reminiscence about the last time you got together. You can also use other corporate links such as common goals.

2 Know the other person's prejudices and attitudes: The more you know about how he or she feels about the topic, the easier it is to get information. It's not terribly hard to find out, in the small-town atmosphere of a company.

3 Seal off distractions: Take only important calls, or move to an off-site meeting place. Make it as comfortable as possible for the person you're interviewing.

4 Take a direct path when:
(a) You feel the person doesn't like you but has no reason to withhold information.
(b) The person is known for discretion.
(c) It is unlikely that there will be direct consequences for the person.
(d) The person has a moral reason to disclose information.

5 Take an indirect path when:

(a) You are asking an employee to compromise his loyalty to other workers.

(b) There is the possibility of self-incrimination.

(c) You are talking to the Dot Cotton of your company, but need the information anyway. Use a smokescreen with gossips. Let them think you're looking for something completely different from your objective. Warning: they are probably more streetwise than you because it's what they do for a living. Gossip is more important than job in many cases.

(d) You expect strenuous objection to your enquiry.

6 Plan your questions: Have a firm idea of what questions you will ask and the sequence you will follow. Questions should be divided into two types: those which solicit information, and those which seek opinions.

7 Know when to shut up: Don't interrupt. Sit quietly and let the person talk.

Instant Review

1 Arrive unencumbered with outerwear, files etc.
2 Try to make the person come towards you, at least part way
3 Give a firm handshake
4 Be equal to your partner
5 Be respectful, whether it's your boss or a member of your staff
6 Replace 'I' with 'you' when you talk
7 Treat your meeting partner as an audience
8 Think tall
9 Don't go in talking
10 Turn your body squarely to your meeting partner
11 Clear your hands before the handshake

Getting your message across eloquently
1 Get right to the point
2 Always ask, 'What would be in it for me if I were this person?'
3 Check for understanding as you go along
4 Always nail the meeting down with concrete follow-up action

To get information
1 Establish rapport immediately
2 Know the other person's prejudices and attitudes
3 Seal off distractions
4 Take a direct path when

  (a) You feel the person you're interviewing doesn't like you and is sceptical about your motives, but has no reason to conceal information
  (b) The person is known for discretion
  (c) There is unlikely to be direct consequence for the person
  (d) The person you're interviewing has a moral reason to disclose

    5   Take the indirect path when
    (a) You are asking an employee to compromise his
        loyalty to fellow workers
    (b) There is the possibility of self-incrimination
    (c) You are talking to a gossip
    (d) You expect strenuous objection to your enquiry

6   Plan your questions and their sequence. Questions are
    either to seek information or to solicit an opinion
7   Know when to shut up

Motivate!

Motivation is getting subordinates to do something – persuasion with concealed weapons, if you like. Often, it's getting staff to do something that isn't their definition of a good time.

Smart bosses see motivation as a form of selling, even though the options of the customer may be few. Good people doing the work while you're at all those meetings is probably the most important corporate asset you have. A chunk of every day should be devoted to their motivation.

Basic motivational meeting tools

1 Make the meetings short: Everything in a motivational meeting has to say, 'I'm the boss'. At other times, you may play other roles, from camp counsellor to fatherly mentor, but when you are motivating your whole tone is business. The brisker the meeting, the better.

2 Keep your own house clean: Are you setting the example they need? You can't call a meeting to talk about office affairs if you're having one, or tardiness if they see you come in late. If you're under pressure to institute policy that goes against the tone of your leadership, tell them that you're in this with them. The company wants it. *We'll* all be in by nine.

3 Don't call a group meeting to motivate a single individual: If you have one or two people flouting your departmental rules, it's a one-to-one meeting, or a one-to-two meeting. Don't address the group.

4 Assume obedience: Time and timing are critical. You'll take the steam out of the presentation if you go into lengthy discussions of consequences. You assume obedience, and let them assume the consequence.

5 Be precise: The usual High Impact rule of precision applies; telling them there's too much time spent around the coffee machine isn't the same as telling them that they can be off station for fifteen minutes and not sixteen.

6 Use short sentences: Here's another old friend from the High Impact barracks. A short sentence puts out clearly what you want. Long discussions are for other meetings. When you motivate, there must never be any doubt where you stand.

7 If the consequence is alien, spell it out: If you're late, you're going to get fired. Ho-hum. But, if you're late and you're going to get five dollars deducted from your pay, and the company has never had such a policy, you must provide complete information, but don't discuss it at length.

8 You won't motivate by insult: Quirky entrepreneurs build fortunes and their tyranny sometimes gets publicized in the press. That's them, not you. Personal insults to staff violate every sound management principle in every book.

9 The past is history: Problem subordinates have a way of developing a new variation of an old disruptive pattern, then sucking the energy out of the meeting when they are asked about it. Old corporate war injuries fester. When you are out to motivate, keep the focus on today.

10 Motivate for a single purpose: Sometimes it's not possible, but when you want your people to do something, bring them in for one thing and leave it at that.

11 Call motivational meetings sparingly

12 Be polite but firm

13 Deal with problems as they occur: Avoid letting personnel problems accumulate. A motivational meeting must have a sense of the now.

14 Remember basic human drives and needs: In short, remember to be reasonable while heading directly for the database of human emotion. We are motivated by feeling not logic, and your task as a motivator is to combine the two. If you want them

115

motivated, they must leave the meeting with their emotions still vibrating.

● **Motivation through inspiration**

1 Show yourself: Personalize your experiences, demonstrating that you have been through what they're experiencing and what you're asking them to experience on your behalf: 'When I joined this company as an eager MBA out of Cranfield, I got to work early the first day . . .'

2 Demonstrate your vulnerabilities: You don't, and shouldn't, confess up there, but you should always be prepared to let your hair down a bit when you want to inspire: 'Computers in my early years were these monstrous machines which took up half a city block. We were supposed to be able to program them with little perforated cards – the term "IBM card" was part of the language. Not *my* language, but *the* language. I was so inept at those cards – '

3 Never tell when you can show: Well-placed and well-produced visuals speak for themselves in a motivational discussion. Instead of telling a group of sales reps about incentives, show them slides or a video of successful employees on a surfboard in Hawaii or driving fancy cars.

4 Audio is a big asset: We all respond to music. You probably know that Springsteen is now more inspirational than 'You'll Never Walk Alone', but what you may not know (and could find out painfully) is that you can't just lift a track and play it in a public place. Music publishing firms get a little unfriendly about that. However, you can get one-shot licensing the way you can get one-day fishing permits. Contact the Mechanical-Copyright Protection Society or the Music Publishers Association in London.

5 Lots of laughter, lots of tears: Pull out all the stops – the time old Jim Matthews decided to drive a fork lift and went through a wall, or the shipping clerk who became an executive because she spotted a design flaw are fodder for your presentation.

6 Relate past successes to ongoing projects: Littlewoods Pools don't make commercials with instant millionaires because the winners are articulate. Anything inspirational must have a 'This *will* happen to you' quality. 'This *can* happen to you' won't do it. There should always be a direct relationship between what has gone before and the successes which are certain to follow.

● **Motivation through intimidation**

You could call this last-resort motivation, because you put it to work only when something's gone very wrong. Unfortunately, every file in your cabinets has a tiny lawyer inside waiting to stampede you with litigation. White-collar crimes and theft of inventory are so widespread that security is one of the growth industries of our time. And if competing companies don't rip off your asset through 'competitor intelligence', some slug on your payroll may be willing to sell a forty-million dollar national secret for a Mercedes convertible and a villa on the beach.

Motivation through intimidation should not be an everyday management style (we all know that it is), but it has its ugly place. Here are a few tips, but remember that you should have a clear and narrow focus for calling the meeting in the first place.

1 Get the goods and get them good: Jobs, careers, personal relationships, self-esteem and other profound human concerns are at stake here. If you have come in with guns, that's life. But if you come in shooting, make sure you're aiming at the real villains.

2 Get the goods fast: Speed is everything. If you don't trust the security department, don't use them. Subordinates survive the same way as executives; they traffic in information. They also eat together, sleep together, and have a loyalty to peers which often transcends the confidential relationships they may be developing with bosses.

3 Who comes is as important as what's said: Make planning the confrontation and who will be present a high priority item. If it's a discreet confrontation, keep the division's town crier away. If you're going to set an example and you want a colourful, juicy blow-by-blow to send chills through the office within fifteen minutes of adjournment, make sure your departmental gossip has a front-row seat.

4 Surprise: Emphasize the urgency by calling a meeting when no one expects it. If Friday afternoons are usually festive, call them in just before they leave for the weekend. Maybe no meetings occur first thing Monday morning. That's a strong time to spring your intimidation on them.

5 Prepare pointed, fact-packed questions: 'Ed, you're an example. Yesterday, you spent only four hours and eight minutes at your desk, and your average time there for the last week was seven minutes less than that. Explain please.'

6 Stick to the issues: You have no case if the meeting deteriorates into name-calling. There are no 'lazy', 'low-life', 'incompetent' or 'inadequate' individuals. Specific desks are never 'pig-pens' or 'stys'.

7 React contrary to their expectations: If you're a Type A hurricane who never sits still, become deadly calm. If you're an avuncular, corporate Bing Crosby always with an encouraging word, blow them right out of the room. Playing against expectation increases a sense of urgency. Just remember that you can do it only once, or once in a while.

8 Talk a little faster than usual: Ask follow-up questions before they're through with their first answers. Demand fast explanations, moving just a flash quicker than they can comfortably abide.

9 End with a dismissal: There's no lingering in an intimidation meeting. You're done and they're to leave fast. They will. If you're in a conference room, walk through the door when you're through, leaving them to absorb the shock.

Instant Review

1 Motivation, for our purposes, is getting subordinates to do something, often something they'd sooner do without
2 Good people are the best asset you have
3 Make motivational meetings short
4 Set a good example, especially with the subject of your motivation
5 Don't use a group forum to motivate one or two people
6 Assume obedience
7 Be precise
8 Use short sentences
9 Spell out alien consequence
10 Never use personal insults
11 The past is history
12 Motivate for a single purpose
13 Call motivational meetings sparingly
14 Be polite but firm
14 Deal with problems as they occur
15 Remember the basic human drives

Motivate through inspiration
1 Show yourself
2 Demonstrate personal vulnerability
3 Never tell when you can show
4 Audio is a big asset
5 Lots of laughter, lots of tears
6 Relate past successes to ongoing projects

Motivation through intimidation
1 Get the goods, get them good
2 Get the goods fast
3 Who comes is as important as what's said
4 Surprise!
5 Prepare pointed, fact-packed questions
6 Stick to the issues
7 React contrary to their expectations
8 Talk a little faster than usual
9 End with a dismissal

Defending Without Appearing Defensive

Someone is always out to put you on the defensive. It can be strategy, management style, a way of communicating, a ploy to impress senior people at the meeting, or an honest, if misguided, method of getting information through devil's advocate role-play. It's never pleasant.

This chapter provides you with several strategies for holding your ground. Criticism often stings, but it's part of the game we play.

1 Criticism is not your enemy: There's a child in all of us waiting either to hide and cry or to strike back when our ideas are criticized. Our education and sophistication never seem adequate to counter our tendency to confuse criticism with personal attack.

Yet we learn from criticism. Many of our most productive actions come from a recognition of areas in our lives which need improvement. If we look back at events that revolutionized our thinking, perhaps even made our careers, we often find they started with someone's constructive advice. Criticism of any kind is never fun, but it loses its bite as time separates us from the circumstances that brought it about. Don't fight an aversion to criticism, but resign yourself to it. Think of the unproductive person who has nothing in his or her life to criticize.

2 Business arguments are not tennis matches: Only one person wins a tennis match. That makes the opponent a loser. Such a simple approach to business arguments is not possible, and if you view each objection to your ideas or actions as a serve, you probably need to evaluate your career goals.

3 Your reaction will be more vividly remembered than your argument: That statement reflects the same principle that applies to any form of delivery, whether you're appearing before a live audience, on television, or in a meeting. How you respond to disagreement will be a permanent part of your corporate image.

4 Don't raise your voice: There are plenty of opportunities to use full voice volume, but dealing with criticism is not one of them. Go home and punch the wall if you must, but in the office stay cool when they don't like your ideas.

5 Listen attentively to the criticism: Listening is often blocked by emotion. Weigh the words carefully as you hear them and, if possible, avoid the temptation to poison your thinking with defensive counter-arguments. Take a beat and just listen.

6 Move forward: Even if some clown is throwing a tantrum and pointing his index finger in your face, lean forward and remain calm. Physically invade your attacker's space while showing no emotion.

7 Validate the criticism: Each person, along with every group of people with common interests, has an aura of position. You can expect a person who interprets scripture literally to be less than thrilled with most religious movies. In the same way, we build assumptions as we go through our business day, and those assumptions are often accurate. Validate the criticism by viewing it from the critic's point of view. People don't get up in the morning counting the ways they can ruin your day.

8 Never use inflammatory language: If you call someone a jerk who wouldn't know a good idea if it ran over his thick head, you have taken that person out of your life for a few years. Your try at cooperation is somewhere between zero and minus five.

Most of us are smart enough to avoid profanity or overtly hostile language. Few of us learn to stop using dismissive or condescending language.

'Bob, I'm afraid your expertise stops pretty short of this problem.'

'I guess you never had direct experience with real estate people, Jane. Let us handle it. Believe me, we speak their language.'

'You're obviously misinformed.'

9 Look for areas of agreement: Somewhere, you and the person criticizing your work are after the same goals. See if you can locate common ground and use it as a reference point.

10 Stick to issues and evidence: The winner always uses the language of reason. Invoke the good of the company, your common goals, or the logic of your position. Keep the evidence unemotional.

11 Store key points of their argument for future use: You may not walk away from a particular confrontation with the upper hand, but you may fortify a future position by taking careful note of the criticism.

12 Seek, and repeat, feedback: As in: 'Let me see if I'm clear here, Joe. You never seek commissions, but you feel you're entitled to one on this deal. You are also aware that our company never pays commissions under your circumstances.'

13 Be open to criticism: Even if you'd like to boil the twerp in his or her body fluids, remain open and conciliatory in tone. Here are some techniques for achieving this:

(a) Negative assertion: You agree with the criticism, sometimes because you've even seen the light. More often, negative assertion is used to take the momentum from the attack.

(b) A conciliatory statement: This comes when you realize you've been a jerk and don't want to say so. Or you've reached a point where you've got to give something to make gains in the negotiation:

'I think I might have overreacted, but you can understand where I was coming from. I'm open to further dicussion before I make up my mind.'

(c) A statement of self-disclosure: Self-disclosure expresses your feelings immediately:

'I'm *very angry* about not seeing those forms before they went out.'

'I am *confident* that we can put this problem behind us and get down to selling our new line.'

(d) Fogging: Acknowledges the criticism while indicating an unwillingness to dwell on it.

'There may be some truth in what you say.'

'That's a thought.'

'I see what you mean.'

14 Don't argue with petty people: You'll find people willing to go to war over whether junior exectives should be given their own stationery. Paper clips and their distribution are a life or death issue for some people. When you encounter this kind of assault, one you feel has no validity, acknowledge the complaint diplomatically and tell the person you don't feel it is germane to today's meeting. Petty people usually aren't going much further. Don't get sucked in by them.

Instant Review

1 Criticism is not your enemy
2 Arguments are not tennis matches
3 Your reaction will be more vividly remembered than the argument you present
4 Don't raise your voice
5 Listen attentively to the criticism
6 Move forward (physically)
7 Validate the criticism
8 Never use inflammatory language
9 Look for areas of agreement
10 Stick to issues and evidence
11 Store key points of their argument for future use
12 Seek, and repeat, feedback
13 Be open to criticism

    (a) with negative assertion
    (b) with a conciliatory statement
    (c) with a statement of self-disclosure
    (d) By fogging

14 Don't argue with petty people

Dealing with a Tough Cast

Meetings produce more characters than a prime time soap opera. As soon as the agenda is handed out, certain individuals slip into their roles and get ready to play out the drama. This chapter introduces strategies for dealing with characters you will work with throughout your career:

Mr Numbers: This person will tell everyone from the CEO to the coffee-trolley attendant that he (usually it's still a he, but that's changing fast) is a *bottom line* man. How much does it cost, how much do we get for the cost? You could be at a high point in your presentation and hear, 'What's the bottom line on this? How are you planning to justify that expense?'
STRATEGY: Have numbers handy, but your approach is that innovation frequently does not have a bottom line. Management is controlling the bottom line. Leadership is seeing the whole picture: 'There's really no bottom line to how much a productive employee produces, Stan. The breakdown is a dollar per division employee per week for six months, or $38,200.'

Rambo: Rambo exists in the foliage of most meetings. He (or just as often she) loves blood, preferably yours. Make a point and he's all over you with fighting words like, 'Stupid', 'That's ridiculous!', 'You're really going to try it that way? You're out of your mind.'
STRATEGY: Your eye contact with Rambo is direct. Show him he can't get you. The worse the attack, the more convinced of your own argument you become because Rambo works hardest to undermine good ideas: 'John, the plan's going to work, but if you feel otherwise, maybe you would like to suggest alternatives.'
Make a rule at the beginning of the meeting that everyone will withhold discussion until the whole idea has been presented. When Rambo attacks, acknowledge and move on. Never let him

influence your next presentation. Don't write with him in mind because he'll never be happy.

Phil Donahue: Ole Phil wants to turn every meeting into a talk show starring him. Every point has a counterpoint, every argument a just and fair counter-argument and what does everyone else think? Come on, speak out here. We've got things to talk about!

STRATEGY: Agendas were made for people like Phil. Remind him that we must stick to the agenda and the ground rules set up at the beginning of the meeting. Confront him afterwards and ask if he wouldn't mind sticking to the topic, expressing his opinion and allowing you to conduct the meeting.

The Capo: This one doesn't command a lot of peer respect because he lives in the exhaust fumes of the boss. He has no opinions of his own, no real innovation, and you wouldn't want him knowing any of your corporate secrets. Most of what he brings up invokes the authority of the boss he serves: 'Well, Lois wouldn't like it. That much I can tell you. She would feel that . . .'

STRATEGY: The Capo survives because he pulls off what he sets out to do; mirror the boss's feelings. You'd better pay close attention and involve him because everything you say is going back immediately to higher authority. Not to worry, though. You can be sure that the leader the Capo represents will move jobs, and this clown will go too.

Dot Cotton: Gossip is fun. We live on it in any field. But in a meeting, hearsay and conjecture are destructive influences. This person will say, 'Well, it doesn't matter what we do because I hear they're planning to move headquarters next year anyway.' This character is worse than Rambo because there's usually a core of truth in her speculation. People listen and your whole momentum is shot.

STRATEGY: Defer the issue. Plants which are supposed to be moved in three months are still in place five years later. Labour problems are solved or avoided. Ask her to verify the information and get back to you. Talk to her privately and tell her that she's not to bring up rumours.

Boo-hoo: Boo-hoo is a malcontent, a whiner who sees everything as impossible. Usually Boo-hoo's career stopped some years back, probably because he or she was too negative. Boo-hoo takes the energy and enthusiasm out of your talk and gets in the way of implementation.

STRATEGY: Never try to appease a malcontent. If she is too senior, or too important, to exclude from meetings, take her aside and ask if she can possibly refrain from negative comments until all sides have given their opinions. Quiet this person down at all costs. You can usually pull it off by acknowledging her value and by showing respect. If not, interrupt her and ask that she follow the agenda. Hold all criticism until the end of the meeting.

Mr/Ms Too-Important-To-Stay: Some fellow executives will test you by arriving late or leaving early. If they're way senior to you, live with it until you can dimplomatically confront. If they're peers, or close to it, you have options.

STRATEGY: Maybe your meetings are too long. Take a look and see if people are arriving late and leaving early because you're combining two or three objectives into a single session.

Assuming that you need no dramatic streamlining of your style, ask the chronically late person why he is tardy. Ask him to come on time because it is important to you. At the beginning of the meeting, ask if everyone can stay the allotted time. This usually eliminates people leaving early. Rushed people sometimes have to be confronted; do so when you're not in a meeting.

Sometimes failing to respect the time allotted to a meeting reflects a loose senior management style. You might be bucking a system you can't control. Change what you can.

Mr and Ms Whisper: When you're presenting, a whisper can have the effect of gunfire. The only strategy is confrontation, in or outside the room. If people are rude enough to whisper, ask them to conduct their business outside. If you have anything to say about the seating, separate the chronic whisperers.

Instant Review

The character	The strategy
Mr Numbers	Have numbers avilable but remember the difference between managing and leading. Innovation has no numbers at times.
Rambo	The worse he gets, the more you should be convinced of the worth of your ideas. Set a rule that ideas are evaluated only after your presentation.
Phil Donahue	Stick to the agenda; confront privately, politely shift away.
The Capo	Just because the person's a jerk, don't assume you can dismiss him or her. When the political climate shifts, this clown will be gone.
Dot Cotten	Keep gossip and hearsay out of meetings at all costs. Ask that rumours be verified. Confront privately.
Boo-hoo	Never appease a whiner; quiet this person down.

The Business Lunch

Your first encounter with the company was probably over lunch with someone. Certainly, you learned how the game is played –

127

who's doing what to whom, with whom, and for whom – at least partly when lunching with your new associates.

One of the most important questions is whether you need a lunch at all. Top people's time is billed out at well over a hundred pounds an hour, and you lose half your body language and sometimes your concentration. If most of the business can be done in a meeting, do it beforehand and use the relaxed luncheon setting to get to know the person.

Lunches, however, are here to stay. The tax laws can change a million times, but business will always be done over lunch or, just as often, dinner. Here are some ways to prepare your luncheon presentations:

1 Have an agenda, however informal: A lunch is a meeting and needs smooth direction. Don't waltz randomly in and out of topics, just because you're in a less formal setting.

2 Jot: Don't whip out the notebook as soon as you're seated, but, when business gets underway and you know your partner is making important points, jot them down. Otherwise you could get back to the office and leave out an important follow-up step.

3 Avoid watering holes: Industry hang-outs are great for career advancement, but you wouldn't conduct important, confidential meetings where your competitor might be a table away. Watering holes are peopled by gossipy staff who have been known to earn extra tips by reporting what they hear.

4 Don't lunch when you're angry with a person: Angry meetings are for closed doors. Controlled tempers can get out of control and you could easily find yourself the butt of insider gossip and jokes after a spectacle.

5 Watch the booze: The so-called 'three martini lunch' was largely a feature of the 1950s, but it's not totally gone. Many executives with clout will down a couple before even thinking about business. If you're not up to his or her capacity, don't be a sport. You won't know what hit you. And if you're not quite part of today's Perrier culture, don't feel a licence to get a buzz on just because you and your buddies have been doing things this way for years.

6 Watch the smoke: If you smoke and your companion doesn't, you're probably going to lose out by smoking at the meal. Even if he or she professes not to mind, a non-smoker always minds. And you know how former smokers go on about how bad cigarettes smell and taste.

7 Work towards a single objective: Maybe you can't make the deal in one meal. Your objective, then, is to fortify the relationship with a follow-up action. Have a specific place you want to be by the time the check is paid.

8 Build follow-up into the lunch: As with any meeting, leave with homework on your part or the other person's, something to continue the transaction, even if things haven't gone especially well.

Instant Review

1. Don't lunch when you can achieve the same in other settings
2. Have an agenda
3. Jot things down
4. Avoid watering holes
5. Don't have lunch when you're angry
6. Watch the booze
7. Watch the smoke
8. Work towards a single objective
9. Build follow-up into the lunch, as with any meeting

Cocktails at Seven, Dinner at Eight

In her book, *Letitia Baldridge's Guide to Executive Manners*, the former Kennedy Administration protocol chief provides perhaps the best example of your number one rule for business social occasions; it's better to ask than take a chance.

An executive was hosting a fancy dinner for his company's clients. When the wine waiter asked him to choose a wine, he did so with authority. So far, so good. But when the waiter returned with the host's choice, the man found himself in a bad spot. He was presented with the cork and didn't know what to do with it. Everyone began to look down as the poor guy stared, baffled, at the cork, hoping maybe it would tell him what happened next. He must have decided to improvise: he bit off the tip of the cork, swirled it around with great authority, and swallowed it. Then he nodded his approval.

Don't be so sure you wouldn't do something equally off-the-wall. Most of us wouldn't eat a cork, but we might try to tip the help at an exclusive club, or say something inadvertently offensive. If you look, and are truthful, there is some version of that cork back there in your corporate life.

If you haven't read Ms Baldridge's book, or any of the dozen or so volumes on corporate protocol, do so. We don't know what we don't know.

All the rules apply to a cocktail party or executive dinner – powervoicing, body language, eye contact, and a careful presentation. These conference room and platform speech techniques will serve you well. Walk in confidently. Entering a business/social occasion is walking onstage, and your posture, body language, and general expression should be the best possible. Is your suit freshly-pressed and are your shoes shined? Have you given the event enough priority, and yourself enough time to freshen up? Here are some tips which apply to cocktail parties and business dinners, but remember always to watch the booze and the smoke:

1 Introduce a junior to a senior person, and a younger to an older: The junior is presented *to* the senior person, the unofficial person *to* the official individual:

'Mrs Stenhouse, I'd like you to meet our executive vice-president, Jerry Moss.'

'Mr Moss, this is my assistant, Tom Morrison.'

2 Know when and when not to use first names: Back in the office, your boss might be just Jerry. When there are civilians around, however, he might want to be called Mr Moss.

You are probably on first-name terms with your secretary, especially in a time of high stress. But when the boss or your peers are around, you would probably get annoyed at being addressed too casually by a staff member. It's a tricky area, but an often overlooked social nuance.

3 Sometimes the occasion isn't for business: You might have been working furiously to get out a report two hours ago, with a crisis-a-minute still pending as you talk to the boss at a cocktail party. The temptation is to blurt things out. Don't; take your cues from the boss.

4 Don't discuss business in mixed company: Many executives have strong feelings about discussing business with their families present. Even when everyone at the party is working towards a common corporate goal, you can blunder by bringing up some office crisis.

5 Don't interrupt

6 Listen: Don't be anticipating your next point as your companion makes hers. Pay attention and comment thoughtfully.

7 If someone makes a pass: The old image of the male boss chasing the secretary is as prevalent and as ugly as ever. But men are now also the objects of sexual advances, especially on the road.

(a) Be direct. 'I really don't want to' is better than being coy and saying 'Not tonight'.

(b) Be pleasant. The boss may have had a drink too many, or a day that was just too long.

(c) Don't blame yourself. Don't question the clothes you wear or the big smile. Some people see sex as a hunt, and you just happen to be in the woods.

(d) Don't mention it later, even in jest.

(e) If it persists, remind your pursuer that there are laws

131

against sexual harassment. They aren't just dusty old statutes, but real, enforceable laws, powerful enough to end careers.

(f) Seek help if it doesn't stop. Chances are, someone higher up finds harassment vulgar. You will almost certainly get some result. You won't be doing the same job but, in today's climate, you will probably survive. It's better than compromising yourself.

8 Be 'other-directed': In a social environment, you have access and informal conversation which you do not have in an office. Pay attention to what the other person feels, and you may indirectly open doors or resolve conflicts which have festered over the months or years.

9 Be sensitive to regional/cultural differences: Not so long ago, American and European businessmen didn't have to worry much about how to act with those of different cultural backgrounds. They usually came to us, were glad to take our money and, what the hell, we were top dogs anyway.

Those days are gone. Today, we have to be extremely sensitive. If you're meeting your counterpart from Bombay, and you think you're going to impress him with the leather interior of your new car, you are wrong. In India, leather is taboo. A barbarian is one who believes reality is defined by his or her experience and vision.

● **Remembering names**

Memory experts construct keys for associating names with faces, and there are courses and books on it. One problem is that the skill is like speed reading. When you come out of the course or put down the book, you're impressive enough to appear on the 'Tonight' show. If you don't practise, the skill fades. Still, it's imperative in business. Here are a few things to remember:

1 Repeat the name when you are introduced: Find an excuse to repeat the name aloud. 'Nice to meet you, Jerry. I'm sorry, I missed your last name.' Get it right there and you'll retain it better.

2 Form a mental image based on the name: Suppose Jerry says his last name is Tatum. Tatum sounds like 'tater' or potato. Think of Jerry as a potato, and Tatum should come back. Any silly association will do.

3 Write down the names you can remember after the party: If you don't do this, the only thing you'll remember about Jerry next time is potato. Jerry Potato. Nice work. But if you write down Jerry Tatum and a little summary of ole Jer, you'll have him next time.

4 Make a picture link of the person and the conversation: Jerry Tatum mentioned his passion for sailing. Now you have a potato in a sailboat. You have fortified the image, and the next time you meet Jerry, you will remind him that you talked about sailing. It will be your secret that you remembered by picturing a potato in a boat.

5 Link the picture with the location: Jerry Potato is now sailing through the Ritz ballroom with a cocktail in his hand.

There is no one right way to use word and face association, but there are many techniques which should work for you. Your system needs to make sense to no one but yourself. Anything is better than just trying to recall names, and the process of linking images is cumbersome only at first. Within a week or so, you'll do it subconsciously and be impressive.

When you remember someone's name and a little about them, you score points immediately. It's worth the effort.

Instant Review

1 Introduce a junior to a senior person, and a younger to an older
2 Know when and when not to use first names
3 Take your conversation cues from the boss
4 Don't discuss business in mixed company
5 Don't interrupt
6 Listen
7 If someone makes a pass, be polite, direct, don't blame yourself and, if need be, take the problem to higher authority
8 Be other-directed in your conversation

To remember names:
1 Repeat a name when you are introduced
2 Form a mental image based on the name
3 Write down names after the party
4 Make a picture link of the person and the conversation
5 Link the picture with the location

The Impromptu Meeting

The brief, non-scheduled meeting usually reflects the management style of a single key individual. Tyrants call them all the time, but so do naturally informal leaders. They are pluses for the following reasons:

1 They save time: When you arrange to visit someone's office, or call that person to yours, you will probably spend a half-hour to execute five minutes of business. If you call or show up, and say, 'Do you have a minute or two right now?' the job gets done without the time drain.

2 They demonstrate vitality and leadership: Leaders move around and radiate energy. They can't live behind a desk.

Managers with limited charisma fly to their desks all the time. They may be efficient, good numbers people, but they certainly aren't going to the top.

Impromptu meetings at, say, a retail outlet, a work station in a factory, or an office away from the mainstream of decision-making geography, show concern for employees. The boss goes to the person. Productivity is probably going up that day.

3 The ideal vehicle for corrective advice: You wouldn't send someone a memo saying, 'I plan to ream you out tomorrow afternoon at three. Be waiting for me in your office.' Presumably, you're the kind of manager who offers constructive advice with a stick as last resort. But when you want to change someone's course do it in an impromptu session.

● **When an impromptu meeting is sprung on you**

Here are five tips if your firm and its key people favour spontaneous meetings:

1 Be physically ready for surprise visits: If you have a boss who shows up unannounced, even once in a while, keep your office tidy and your staff alert. Don't get caught partying at ten in the morning because it's Darcy's birthday, and we all love Darcy. Those events, if they're for the office at all, are for the end of the day.

2 Be substantively ready: You always owe the boss something. You promised a report by Wednesday, or that the Cleveland office would get the report by air express. If you are in an impromptu meeting environment, have these promises of follow-up ready and accessible.

3 Don't be afraid to buy time: If a deadline has been chasing you all morning, speak up and buy yourself some time. Be direct and respectful, but assertive in the larger interests of the company. There's nothing wrong with delaying fifteen minutes if that's what you need.

135

4 Know your data and who's responsible for access: You need someone nearby who can produce reports, printouts, memos and other paperwork immediately. People who can get their hands on crucial information quickly are impressive.

5 Sound like you mean business: Your vocal tricks, body language, eye contact, and all the High Impact skills should be consciously activated. This isn't bar conversation but a real presentation, however spontaneous.

Instant Review

Impromptu meetings, though favoured by tyrants, serve many purposes:

– They save time
– They demonstrate vitality and leadership
– They are the ideal vehicle for corrective advice

1 Be physically ready for them
2 Be substantively prepared
3 Don't be afraid to buy some time
4 Know how to gain access to your data quickly
5 Sound like you mean it

The Eloquence of Saying Nothing

Get used to it, if you haven't already. Someone is always going to try to get a quote out of you, so he can either use it against you, or put it to work for him: 'Well, I was talking to Masterson down in production, and he agreed with me that . . .'

Or, one of your beloved colleagues wants to provoke you into corridor battle: 'I think Roberts is out of his league in the home office, don't you agree?'

There are many times in corporate life when the most eloquent thing you can do is to be silent. These ten occasions are mainly for dealing with people at or near your corporate level. They apply to bosses and subordinates, but with Kremlinesque shades of subtlety.

Say nothing when:

1 Someone says something which appears to have no purpose but provocation, especially in or before an important meeting: 'You probably aren't too familiar with the ins and outs of employee relations, since you never actually supervise anyone.'

2 You are pressured to take sides in a dispute which has no effect on your area of responsibility.

3 You are asked for an opinion when you haven't studied the facts.

4 You are clearly being pressured to express an opinion which may later be used against you.

5 When you are the target of a perfunctory apology which is not an apology at all, but an excuse for inexcusable behaviour: 'Hey, sorry about that, but I had my reasons. I'm sure you understand.'

6 Whenever someone makes a fool of himself and tries to drag you down too. 'I suppose Mr Kowalski never did anything like this. Mr Kowalski never offends anyone, does he?'

7 When someone asks you a question he has no business asking: 'Just between you and me, did you get that extra fifty thousand when you came over?'

8 When someone interrupts your presentation with an irrelevant comment when you are in the middle of a point. Stare at him briefly and continue.

9 Use silence as a warning shot when you are the subject of bad manners. Say nothing, pause, stare and continue with precisely-articulated syllables for a few beats. He's on notice; next time, you'll zap him.

10 When you stumble on an improper situation such as a dozing boss, an embracing couple or an unpleasant exchange.

Instant Review

Silence is its own eloquence. Say nothing when:

1   You are deliberately provoked in or just before an important meeting
2   You are pressured to take sides in an argument which does not affect your area of responsibility
3   You are asked for an opinion when you don't know the facts
4   You are pressured to give an opinion which may later be used against you
5   You are the target of a meaningless apology which is really an excuse
6   When someone is making a fool of himself and tries to drag you down with him
7   When someone asks you a question which is none of his business
8   When you are rudely interrupted for no relevant purpose
9   As a warning shot to a corporate bully
10 When you stumble on something improper

Listening: The Ultimate Weapon

Be a better listener. Listening is such a powerful tool that you could run an ad in an adventure magazine promising:

SECRET WORD REVEALED FOR
MONEY AND POWER BEYOND IMAGINATION.
SEND £10
AND LIVE WELL FOREVER

If you ran that ad, then sent the word 'listen' to those who always want any easy path to wealth and power, you would be attacked for shameless exploitation. Some chap with political ambitions would see you in the stocks. But you would be innocent. Study after study shows that misunderstanding between people occurs because we don't know how to listen. Or we won't even if we know how. Choose the five biggest business hassles you've had in the past year. Think about what went wrong:

'Oh, you meant *shipping*? Why didn't you say shipping? I thought you meant receiving.'

'You never said that. What you said was . . .'

'I never said that. What I said was . . .'

'I could swear you said, "buy a truck", so I bought a truck. If you didn't say, "buy a truck", what did you say?'

'I said don't buy a truck.'

Mastery of listening skills is difficult. The hardest part is that it's a task we don't think we have to learn, so we don't take it seriously. Take it seriously.

Here are some tips for effective listening:

1 Look directly at the speaker, especially in one-to-one meetings.

2 Look for an old curiosity: 'I've always wondered about that,' should be your response to the talk. There are many things you've wondered about, and there is a good-to-excellent chance that the speaker will address one of your cobweb-covered curiosities.

3 Guess where the speaker is going next: This is like experimenting with electricity. A little bit is fun, but if you go beyond your ability, you'll be zapped. Focus only on the next point, not five or six items down the road. If you can anticipate the next topic or subtopic, you'll have the information more firmly planted.

4 Don't interrupt – it's just plain rude.

5 Repeat the main points to yourself: It doesn't take a doctorate to discover a speaker's main points. Each time you hear an inflection which signals a piece of information important to the speaker, slow your thinking down long enough to verbalize the thought.

6 Recapitulate throughout the body of the presentation: Either you can do this or you can't. Some find the task as enjoyable as chewing on cardboard. Recapitulation means that you've stopped listening because you have put your mind on recapping. Others can count off a speaker's main points in a few minutes. In any event, it won't hurt to make the effort, which pays big dividends.

7 Keep charged words in their places: If the speaker's phraseology annoys you, it's probably intended to do so. Don't let it keep you from hearing the rest of the argument.

8 Mesh ideas with the facts: Ideas are often more important than dry individual facts. Keep the bigger picture in mind and put the facts in perspective.

9 Don't be quick to call the subject uninteresting: To the dullard, everything is uninteresting. If you write the presentation off at the beginning, you might miss a real education.

Instant Review

Good listening is one of the great High Impact speaking skills. Unfortunately, most people fail to develop their ability to listen.

1 Look directly at your speaker
2 Seek out an old curiosity
3 Guess where the speaker is going next
4 Don't interrupt
5 Repeat the main points to yourself to keep your mind from wandering
6 Recapitulate
7 Keep charged words in their place
8 Mesh ideas with the facts; keep the bigger picture in mind
9 Don't be quick to call the topic uninteresting

The Association for Management Education and Development (AMED) is the only voluntary association of professionals in the UK whose work focuses exclusively on management training, education and organization development. Membership is open to anyone involved in this significant field of work. AMED's fast growth in recent years has created a lively membership of interested people in business, government, voluntary organizations, academic institutions and managerial consultancy.

The main aim of AMED is to promote high standards of management performance so that people in organizations and communities can work with greater effectiveness. Members are therefore encouraged to meet and collaborate to improve their own professional capabilities. Activities include evening and one-day meetings, and three- to four-day events held all over the UK and in Europe. These are designed to provide members with different developmental opportunities for the various stages of their careers. They also enable members to extend their knowledge and skills, to keep in touch with frontier thinking on management, and to exchange ideas and experience.

Free publications are sent to members. These include *MEAD (Management Education and Development)*, a journal which has three issues a year and contains articles on current management training and development; frequent focus papers on topical issues; and a monthly newsletter.

For further information, contact:

AMED
Premier House
77 Oxford Street
London W1
01-439 1188

Keep Going For It!

Living the Life of an Entrepreneur

Victor Kiam is going for it again! Just in case you thought it might be time to take it easy, the king of entrepreneurs has put together a second colourful cocktail of advice and anecdote to keep you up and running with the best of them.

Victor Kiam is known to millions as 'the man who bought the company' – the man who liked the Remington shaver so much that he bought the entire corporation that made it. He took a loss-maker and made it profitable – then wrote *Going For It!*, the bestseller that explained how it was done. End of story? By no means, Victor Kiam is an entrepreneur, a man who knows that if you stop developing you're not just standing still – you're going backwards.

In *Keep Going For It!* Victor Kiam explains how to succeed as an entrepreneur – and then keep on succeeding. Whether your pitch is a market stall or a conglomerate's boardroom the principle is the same – recognize your potential, maximize that potential and keep on maximizing that potential. Just what should be done when it seems every tangible asset's been exhausted and a project still won't rise off the ground? What happens when it seems that every potential buyer for your brilliant new idea just can't see past the first trifling hurdle? What can be done when a new scheme falls flat – even crashes into failure? Who should win when your home life and your business life are set on a collision course? *Keep Going For It!* offers hardnosed solutions to each of the above – and more – with specific examples drawn from a lifetime of successful risk-taking.

If you're a true entrepreneur then business is *the* great adventure – but only if you *Keep Going For It!*

FONTANA PAPERBACKS

The 100 Best Companies to Work for in the UK

Bob Reynolds

Foreword by John Harvey-Jones

The 100 Best Companies to Work for in the UK is an incisive and most revealing guide to the country's key employers. From the massive multinational to the smallest family firm, these companies have one thing in common. They are all excellent employers.

In the most comprehensive survey of employment in British industry ever undertaken, more than 1500 companies have been evaluated on eight primary criteria:

- Pay
- Benefits
- Promotion
- Training
- Working Environment
- Ambience
- Equal Opportunities
- Financial Performance

A team of researchers has combed the length and breadth of the UK to find 100 excellent workplaces. See how your company performs. Rate it against the competition. Test its scale of benefits against an average top-100 best employer.

Does it match up to Marks & Spencer, which has the best pay and benefits package in the retail sector? Do its industrial relations compare with Vickers Defence Systems, which had one of the worst employment records on Tyneside a few years ago and now has one of the best? Read how staff and management achieved the turnaround.

Whether you are a company chairman, or in search of your first job, this book is essential reading. It also shows how business can boom when management offer inspired leadership and treat their employees with respect.

FONTANA PAPERBACKS

Fontana Paperbacks
Non-fiction

Fontana is a leading paperback publisher of non-fiction. Below are some recent titles.

- ☐ The Motor Makers *Martin Adeney* £4.50
- ☐ Keep Going For It! *Victor Kiam* £3.99
- ☐ The Eloquent Executive *William Parkhurst* £3.99
- ☐ How to Pick People for Jobs *Viv Shackleton* £3.99
- ☐ Getting the Best *Buck Rodgers* £3.99
- ☐ Making It Happen *John Harvey-Jones* £3.99
- ☐ The 100 Best Companies to Work for in the UK
  Bob Reynolds £5.95
- ☐ All This and Work Too *Dr Maryon Tysoe* £3.95

You can buy Fontana paperbacks at your local bookshop or newsagent. Or you can order them from Fontana Paperbacks, Cash Sales Department, Box 29, Douglas, Isle of Man. Please send a cheque, postal or money order (not currency) worth the purchase price plus 22p per book for postage (maximum postage required is £3).

NAME (Block letters) _____

ADDRESS _____

_____

_____

While every effort is made to keep prices low, it is sometimes necessary to increase them at short notice. Fontana Paperbacks reserve the right to show new retail prices on covers which may differ from those previously advertised in the text or elsewhere.